MOTHMAN DYNASTY

CHICAGO'S WINGED HUMANOIDS

LON STRICKLER

BEYOND THE FRAY
Publishing

BEYOND THE FRAY

Publishing

For my friends and colleagues.

ACKNOWLEDGMENTS

I want to thank the Chicago Phantom Task Force for their contributing research and investigation. I also want to thank all the eyewitnesses who came forward and allowed me to share their experiences.

Special recognition needs to be given to the researchers, friends and colleagues whose support has been invaluable. They include, and are notlimited to: Manuel Navarette - UFO Clearinghouse, Tobias Wayland and Emily Wayland – The Singular Fortean Society, Rosemary Ellen Guiley, Butch Witkowski, Ash Staunton, Timothy Renner, Vance A. Nesbitt, Nicole Tito Grajek, Billy Bantz, Rob Shaw, Stan Gordon, Jamie Brian, Brett Butler, Sean Forker, Jeffrey and Krystle Drenning, JC Johnson, Ken Gerhard, Linda Godfrey, Albert Rosales, as well as all the 'Phantoms & Monsters' readers.

Please be aware that most of the eyewitness accounts in this book are written by ordinary people. Some text has been changed; but for the most part, it's been left unedited and as received. Thanks for your understanding.

Lon Strickler

www.phantomsandmonsters.com

INTRODUCTION

As I begin writing the narrative of the 'Chicago Phantom' saga, I have just documented the 40th witness sighting since late March 2017. The questions about this winged being still exist 5 months after the initial report. What is it? Where is it coming from? Why now? Is there a reason why the sightings are occurring in the general Chicago metro area?

This current group of winged humanoid sightings is probably the largest since the Mothman encounters in the vicinity of Point Pleasant, WV during 1966-67. Those sightings have become legendary, namely because the Mothman was seen as a harbinger of catastrophe, after the collapse of the Silver Bridge on the evening of December 15, 1967. The bridge spanned the Ohio River between Point Pleasant, WV and Gallipolis, Ohio and the disaster took the lives of 46 people.

The fact that most people have referred to the subjects of these sightings in Chicago as a 'Mothman' is understandable. As with all winged humanoid sightings and encounters that occurred before and after the Mothman of Point Pleasant events, there may be a chance that these variously described beings could be related in some way or another. Are these winged humanoids the progeny of the Mothman?

On June 7, 2017, M.J. Banias wrote an article at Mysterious Universe titled 'Chicago's Current Mothman Flap; "A Warning," Says Expert.' In his article Banias described the ongoing wave of Mothman- type sightings in and around the city. The article quoted me:

> "There are many opinions as to why these sightings are occurring, including a general feeling that unfortunate events may be in the city's future. (...) At this point, I feel that this being may be attempting to distinguish a connection between locales within the city and future events. The witnesses have been very steadfast with what they have seen, and refuse to embellish on their initial descriptions. Each witness has had a feeling of dread and foreboding, which I believe translates into a warning of some type."

I somewhat regret making that speculative statement so early in the investigation. Eventually the quote may prove to be true, but I want to let the facts and evidence determine what these winged humanoids really are. It is my opinion that the good people of Point Pleasant were so shocked and distraught over the deaths that they wanted to find something to blame for the collapse. Thus we have the theory that the Mothman was a portent of destruction. Unfortunately, a large number of Chicagoans now fear that they are in line for a similar fate.

The presence of unknown winged beings is probably as old as the human imagination; but after reading and listening to hundreds of eyewitness accounts over the past four decades, I have concluded that these beings are much more than fantasy.

This book will examine the witness accounts and the investigators' thought processes, as these incidents were brought to our attention. There is reasonable expectation that several more reports will come to light while this narrative is being written. It's a work in progress... but we're determined to find the truth.

A BIT OF HISTORY

FLYING humanoid sightings and encounters are not a new occurrence in the Chicago metro area. A few reports have been forwarded to me in the past, even though I have no way of knowing if those incidents are related to the current group of sightings.

The following account is as chilling as I have ever read in reference to a flying humanoid encounter. The witnesses were of Navajo descent, who had moved to Chicago a year or so before this incident occurred. The writer was an acquaintance of the family:

"I live in Chicago, and my friend's mom told him about this creature. Well, he told me that in 2005, his mom and dad were driving in the city and that they noticed a giant bat-like creature following them at high speed. Obviously they didn't believe their eyes at what they saw, but luckily they sped up the car and got far away from the creature. His father was so shocked, that he just about smashed the car into a tree.

They later stopped the car and discussed about what that thing was. While they were talking they once again noticed the creature flying towards them. His father started the car, but the creature was closely upon them. Then without any hesitation, it smashed itself into the windshield. It was like it didn't see the window. Then it broke the glass on the front passenger side door. My friend's mom was sitting there while it tried to put its claws into her arm. His dad had a glass bottle which he cracked into the creature's head. It fell on the ground and they drove away as fast as they could.

They assumed that they had gotten rid of the creature. When they arrived home, it was apparent that my friend's mom was injured. After helping his wife out of the car, his dad went back to close the car door. Then suddenly, the creature again appeared at a tremendous speed and attacked his mom. It attempted to grab her and fly away. But quickly, his dad beat the creature with a stone. It eventually took off and disappeared into the dark sky.

When the creature tried to take his mom away, she got a closer look at it. After all this happened and her being injured, she told her husband that, "It's a kind of extinct creature. It had long sharp nails, a very scary face, glowing eyes and sharp teeth." His mother looked on internet to see what the creature was. They were only thinking about one creature; a Skinwalker, because they were familiar with that creature because of their culture. It's a witch that can transform into a half animal/half human. After a lot of research, they eventually discovered that the creature closely resembled only one being, The Mothman.

Since then, they always avoid dark places and those areas where other people don't frequent. They still believe that the creature will return and attack them.

After I heard about the incident from my friend, I thought he was lying; but when I heard this story from his mom, I now believe it occurred. Even if this winged creature *exists, I will not truly believe it until I see it with my own eyes."*

This is a harrowing encounter that involved an attack. There have not been any bodily injuries inflicted by these winged beings during the current flap of sightings. But there have been a few very 'personal' encounters where the witnesses were affected emotionally and physically.

The Chicago/Lake Michigan area, as well as most of the upper Midwest, has had its share of bizarre events related to cryptids and other supernatural phenomena. But none compare in scope with the current group of winged being sightings in and around Chicago.

———

IN THE LATE summer and early autumn of 2011, there were 3 reports of large winged beings in Chicago. I believe that these sightings were a nexus for what was to occur in 2017, since the descriptions were fairly similar to the more recent witness reports.

On 10/13/2011, a report was forwarded to UFO Clearing-house in reference to an incident that occurred on 8/22/2011:

"I'm from the southwest suburbs of Chicago. My wife and I traveled into Chicago to take care of some business. On the way back we took a cruise through my old neighborhood just to check it out and to see what had changed. We were driving west on 63rd St. and approaching Pulaski Rd.

I then remembered the giant Indian statue that was on the roof of this tobacco store (that's what it was when I was a kid; it's something else now) on the northwest corner of 63rd and Pulaski Rd. So when my wife and I were driving near this

Indian statue at about 2:oopm, I decided to take a picture of it. I had just bought a new smart phone and I wanted to check out how good the camera would work.

So I got out of the car took about four pictures of this Indian statue. We left and went home. Later that night I went to look at the pictures I took. When I was checking these photos out, in one of the pictures I noticed the object that was on the backside of Indian. At first I didn't think anything of it, I figured it was plane or something. But just for the heck of it, I enlarged it. It looked something similar to a bird or a bat, but then again it doesn't. So I have no idea what it could be. I was reluctant to send it in because I figured there was some explanation for what it is. But then I thought it still qualifies as a UFO, because I never seen anything like it before and don't know what it could be."

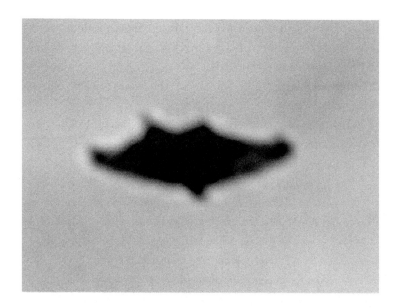

The photograph produced a moderate stir within the cryptozoology community, because it was an indication that cryptid winged beings may actually exist.

ON SEPTEMBER 30, 2011, UFO Clearinghouse received a second witness report of an unknown being within the Chicago city limits:

> *"These are the events as they happened on Friday, September 30, 2011, in the area around Miller Park in the University Park neighborhood in Chicago; approximately 1 block from the main campus of the University of Illinois at Chicago.*
>
> *Things began like any normal Friday night. A couple of friends and myself were going to go out to have a few drinks at a local bar. As I got to my apartment, I jumped into the shower to start getting ready while my roommate went to her room to*

get ready. I finished and walked out of the bathroom to my room and started to get dressed.

I then heard my roommate scream loudly. I dropped what I was doing and ran to her room to see if she was all right. I walked in to see her cowering in the corner of her room, white as a ghost and shaking. She was babbling hysterically, saying that something was looking in at her from the window. I looked toward the window and didn't see anything other than the light coming from the other apartments across the court yard. I asked what she had seen and tried to tell her that she might have been mistaken. We live on the third floor of a five-story apartment building and there is nothing outside the window but a thirty foot drop straight down to the courtyard below.

My roommate was hysterical and scared out of her wits. I helped her to the living room and sat her on the couch. I then went to my room to put on a robe or a nightshirt on since I was only in my underwear. My roommate didn't want to be left alone and actually followed me and waited as I put on a robe and joined her in the living room. After about 20 minutes of calming her down, she finally told me what she had seen in her window.

She stated that she was getting dressed and when she turned to face the mirror on her dresser, she saw a pair of orange eyes staring at her from the window. She turned around to see two brightly lit orange eyes looking out at her. These eyes were attached to a creature that was staring back at her through the window. My friend lost it and started screaming hysterically and backed herself into the corner. She said she was filled with this overwhelming feeling of complete and total terror, and felt like the creature was looking at her as though she was prey. She said she felt like a rabbit that was about to be pounced upon by an eagle.

I tried to rationalize with her, telling her it could have been an optical illusion, or maybe it was the jitters from a week of hard studying. She dismissed everything, saying that she had seen what she had seen. As I sat there comforting her, my cell phone rang from my room. I got up and ran to my room and snatched it from my dresser top and answered it. It was my boyfriend and one of his buddies and they were talking a mile a minute. It sounded like they were out of breath. As I tried to get him to slow down, I walked past my roommates open door and to my absolute horror, I saw a pair of glowing red eyes, looking through the window right at me!

They stared at me for about three to four-seconds before whatever it was abruptly left. Like my friend, I totally lost it and screamed at the top of my lungs and sprinted to the living room. My boyfriend was now screaming into the phone; "What's wrong, what's wrong?"

Within two minutes, he and his best friend were pounding on the door to our apartment, followed shortly thereafter by one of our neighbors who had heard us screaming. Once we assured the neighbors that we were fine and that they did not have to call the CPD for us, we shut the door and I immediately lost it when my boyfriend held me.

We told him what my roommate had seen in the window and that whatever it was had come back again, that's when I had seen it. He then began to tell us that he and his buddy were on their way to our apartment to pick us up when they had seen what they described as a large bat with large glowing eyes. It was perched on top of a basketball hoop in the neighborhood park. They stated that it saw them and quickly ascended into the air with an audible 'whoosh.'

He stated that there were about six people in the park and all of them had seen it when it had taken off. He said that there was no way anyone could have missed it, because it was about six to seven feet tall, dark grey to black and those eyes glowed with the intensity of two glowing embers.

He said that they saw it easily when it took off and headed away from the park due to both the lights of the city as well as the nearly full moon that night. They lost sight of the creature after about five-seconds, that's when he picked up the phone and called me. He then said that when they heard me start screaming, they sprinted the block and a half to the apartment.

Needless to say, none of us went out that night and my boyfriend and his buddy stayed with us through the weekend. My roommate refused to go back to her room till it was well after daylight, she closed and locked the window and drew the blinds shut. She says that it's the only way that she felt secure to be in there after dark.

"I'm still wary about coming home or going out after dark; even though I know I have to do it for both school and work. I hope that whatever it was, it was sufficiently scared off by two frantic screaming college students and that I hope that I never see it again. I don't think that neither I nor my roommate will ever be the same again after this." There is one interesting fact. "My boyfriend told me when I saw him on Tuesday that a few students around the campus (University of Illinois/Chicago) had been talking about a large bat that some people had seen on Friday night. A lot of the people who spoke about it were really spooked by it."

Those multiple sightings are very similar to what several of the recent witnesses are describing, especially the red eyes and the sudden acceleration into the air.

APPROXIMATELY TWO WEEKS after the Miller Park incident, another report of a large bat-like being surfaced at UFO Clearinghouse:

"I am currently attending the University of Chicago and I wanted to respond to the informational flyers about recent events involving the large bat-like creatures.

I was enjoying an evening with my girlfriend and taking a well-deserved break from my studies. We decided to go out and enjoy the unusually warm weather that we were having and go for a walk.

As we walked toward a community park near the campus, we were talking about our classes when a commotion amongst a group of people caught our attention. As we looked toward the group of about four to five people, something caught my eye and I looked up to see this thing fly overhead. It looked like a man; it looked like a man with wings!

It flew about ten to twelve feet above us and was perfectly silhouetted against the evening sky. In all honesty, it looked like an immensely oversized Sugar Glider, the kind I would see back home in Tasmania. It had the rough shape of a Sugar Glider, but its eyes were nothing like the soft eyes of the animal. They glowed red! We saw it for about four-seconds before it disappeared from view. At first I thought I saw a man in a hang glider, but it was those bloody eyes that made me think otherwise!

I at first thought of ringing someone, but I didn't want them to think I had gone crazy. To say that I was gobsmacked would have been an understatement."

I had later verified that flyers had been distributed at a few college campuses in and around Chicago. As far as I know, this was the last report of this bat-like being in 2011.

Manuel Navarette at UFO Clearinghouse, paranormal investigator Joshua P. Warren and Phantoms & Monsters were just of few of the websites reporting and commenting on the sightings.

We never dreamed that this phenomenon would rebound in the Windy City.

2

OZ PARK

(NO 'FLYING MONKEY')

PEOPLE EVOKE THE WORD 'KARMA' when it involves someone's destiny or fate, usually the result of an undesirable deed. But on the other hand, fate can bring good fortune; and a bit of 'good karma' befell Manuel Navarette on April 10, 2017. That is the day that UFO Clearinghouse received the first indication that another unknown winged being had arrived in Chicago. It only seems fitting that this report reached him, since he was the recipient of the three witness accounts in 2011, and that he never wavered on the statements.

The following account, that occurred on April 7, 2017, was forwarded to UFO Clearinghouse:

> *"I'm writing this out after taking a day or two to really, really think out if I wanted to report this and tell others of what I saw the other night in Oz park here in Chicago. I finally decided that writing this out and submitting it would be therapeutic to me and might hopefully help identify what it was that I saw and maybe help someone else avoid the same thing.*
>
> *I live in the Lincoln Park neighborhood in the city of Chicago and live about one and a half blocks from Oz Park.*

When the weather is nice, I usually go outdoors and to the park to jog and walk my dog. The night of April 7 was no different, it was mild and the cold weather had finally subsided so I decided to give the treadmill a break and go outside to jog and let the dog get some fresh air. As I came to the corner of Burling St. and Webster Avenue where I cross the street to the park, my dog began acting very peculiar, like she didn't want to go to the park. This is very strange as usually my dog goes absolutely nuts when we go to the park and has the time of her life running and sniffing. On this particular evening, she acted like she was mortified to cross the street and enter the park.

As we crossed the street and came up to the area where the basketball courts are located and the start of the trail that goes around and through the park, my dog was practically being dragged as she resisted wanting to continue. After much effort, I finally got her to finally cooperate and begin the walk. I started walking east toward the Oz Garden, a route that is my usual when I come here to walk or to jog. As we walked toward the garden, I noticed that many of the birds you usually hear in the park were all but silent and that the only noise you could hear was the usual city noise from the surrounding neighborhood.

As we rounded the sidewalk to head south with the garden to my left, I heard what could only be described as the flapping of wings. I really didn't give it a second thought as I assumed it would be some passing Canadian Geese that I've seen in the park recently. As we came toward the clearing where you would find the baseball fields, something caught my eye and what I saw still scares the crap out of me. I saw a large man, probably seven feet or taller standing on the ground.

It was solid black, but what really stood out were the large, and I do mean large pair of wings that were folded behind him. These wings stood taller than the man by at least a foot and a half and jutted out of his back. I could not see its face as it had been turned away from me and probably didn't notice me at first. It finally turned and noticed me. I saw the bright, ruby red eyes that appeared to glow from within. It was at this time that it turned and faced me and I got to see what it really looked like.

It was about seven feet tall, and instead of clothes, it looked like a giant half man, half bird kind of thing. It reminded me of the character Birdperson from the show Rick and Morty, only a LOT scarier! This thing stared at me for about fifteen-seconds, which felt like an eternity and then in a loud whoosh it unfurled its wings and screeched really loud, and jetted into the air. These wings looked almost bat-like and were at least 10 feet across from tip to tip. I felt like this thing could see right through me, read me, it knew what I was thinking, like it could stare right into my very soul. It was the most terrified I have ever been in my life. It rose into the air like a bullet and I heard it screech once more before losing it from my view as it rose above the trees and possibly the buildings. It was at that time that I realized that I had yet to scream or react in any way. I was just numb, numb from my head to my toes. I finished my walk early and walked home, all the while trying to see if I could see it again once I got to the street.

It was the scariest thing I have ever experienced and it lead me to look up giant mutant birds online and eventually came to sites talking about similar sightings that other people have had and eventually to where I could post and report my own sighting. I don't want you to think that I'm crazy. I'm just a normal person who had a weird and strange experience. I do not abuse drugs or take any kind of hallucinogens or anything like that.

I know what I saw was real and that I saw it in Oz Park, in Chicago, Illinois. I don't want publicity at all, I just want to *tell my story and to warn others who might jog or walk the trails of Oz Park. I never felt like I was in any real kind of danger, if I did not provoke it. But, I felt that this creature could have ripped me limb for limb if I had approached it or threatened it in any way. Maybe it was passing through like the Canadian Geese do when they are migrating. Either way, I hope that we never get to meet face to face again. Thank you."*

When Manuel contacted me and told me what was seen, I initially thought that this may be a hoax. But after I took the time to read the account and examine the testimony, it was apparent to me that this witness had encountered a similar being; the same type of being that had been reported in 2011.

As always, Manuel gave me permission to post the account on Phantoms & Monsters. He stated that he was going to interview the witness as soon as possible. The following information was gleaned from the interview.

Investigator's Follow-up:

"I managed to make contact with the witness as to the original sighting, and after some discussion over the phone, we were able to clear some time to meet and discuss the sighting in detail.

The witness, who did not wish to be identified due to professional reasons, agreed to be interviewed about her experience as long as no revealing information was given. For that purpose, I will call the witness "Tammy" in lieu of her real name.

Background: Tammy is an educated professional who has

lived in the Oz Park neighborhood for over 10 years and after I asked a few basic questions, she appears to be a credible witness with no need to propagate a hoax. The Oz Park area is located in the Lincoln Park neighborhood of Chicago's south side and is about four blocks from The Lincoln Park Zoo and the Lake Michigan shoreline, and about 10 blocks south of Wrigley Field. The area is mostly condos and apartment buildings. The neighborhood is mixed race and mostly upper middle-class professionals and students attending nearby DePaul University. The park is a landmark and tourist attraction for its "Wizard of Oz" theme park and statues, and is popular among the many residents for various activities.

The Sighting: The witness stated that when she came to the spot where she saw the creature, it was looking away from her. It was not until it turned its head that it took notice that she was there. The dog (a Jack Russell Terrier) which she stated is normally very protective of her, was cowering behind her and whimpering. I note the breed of the dog, because a Jack Russell is a breed that is only recommended for advanced dog owners due to high energy, fearless nature, and very prey attack driven. This is a dog that is not easily intimidated and to reduce one to a cowering manner, leaving its master in a vulnerable position, is quite unusual.

The witness stated that she never felt as if she were in any immediate danger, as long as she stayed where she was. The witness reported that the creature's eyes glowed unnaturally, as if illuminated from within and never seemed to blink. She reported that even though the creature was mainly black in color, the wings did have some gray to them (as best as she could see) and did not look like it had feathers like an owl's wings, but appeared leathery and bat-like. She stated that the top part of the wings seems to rise at least a foot higher than the head of the creature and were folded behind it.

After staring at her for approximately fifteen-seconds, it unfurled its wings; which appeared to be about eight to ten feet from wingtip to wingtip. The wings looked to be made of a membrane, not unlike a bat's wings. The creature leaped into the air with minimum effort and was gone within seconds. The screech sounded like an owl, only louder and raspier. She noted that the creature was above the treetops within seconds and out of sight just as fast. When asked if there was a possibility that others could have seen it, she stated that unless they were looking right at it, they could have missed it. Once above the trees, it would have been lost due to trees and buildings blocking the view, as well as light pollution making it practically invisible. She noted that in the city, most people would have been too busy looking at their phones or talking to one another or aware of their immediate surroundings to notice anything flying overhead.

When asked why she never attempted to take a photograph with her phone, the witness stated that she was frozen in place and that the thought of grabbing her phone (which was in her pocket) never occurred to her. She feels that part of the fear she felt was due to some unknown influence the creature might have had over her; a possible defense mechanism she hypothesized.

The witness states that since her encounter, she has resumed her jogging in the park in the early evenings when the weather permits. She did state that her dog has been very reluctant to continue visiting the park and the last time she took him along, he had to be coaxed into completing the run.

In conclusion, I feel that the witness had a credible sighting and believes that what she saw was real. I walked along the running trails of the park and saw the spot where she reported the sighting. I believe her statement that the creature would have been lost from sight once it was above the treetops *making it difficult to see. Even though many of the trees had minimum to no foliage, they are bunched tightly enough to provide a canopy that would make it difficult to track anything in the air from the perspective of the park.*

The description of the creature fits those of the "Mothman" that have been reported throughout the world. If this is the same creature or a different variant, it remains as speculation. Identifying the creature only through eyewitness accounts, and no physical or photographic evidence, would be very difficult."

THE DESCRIPTION by this witness is very similar to the 'Mothman-like' being reports that I and others have received over the years. I don't sense that there was any embellishment in Tammy's statement and subsequent interview; an aspect that Manuel and I have noticed from the witnesses who we have interviewed since the beginning of this flap.

Though we really didn't expect that more witnesses come forward, we could only hope that this winged being would make itself known again.

3

'THE BIGGEST FREAKING OWL I HAVE EVER SEEN!'

ONE WEEK after the Oz Park encounter, a report surfaced on the MUFON CMS, describing a flying humanoid that was seen by multiple witnesses at the loading docks of the Chicago International Produce Market:

Chicago, IL - 2017-04-15: "I arrived for work at 2am at the Chicago International Produce Market just off S. Damen Ave. As I walked across the parking lot, a bunch of guys (four to five guys) were staring up at the sky. I looked up and saw the biggest freaking owl I have ever seen! I'm 6'2" and I'm guessing this thing was at least a foot taller than me. It was completely black except for it having bright yellowish/reddish eyes like a cat. It perched there for a minute or two staring at everyone before shooting up into the sky and disappearing. It made everyone feel very uneasy and only took off after some guys threw some rocks at it. It had wings on it like an owl, only bigger and you could hear it flap those wings when it took off.

It made this sound as it took off and as it flew away, it sounded like a truck's brakes when they are burned out. It flew up and flew a wide circle, making that sound once more, and then flew off in the direction of the Stevenson Expressway. We stood around and looked for it for a few minutes, but it never came back.

I'm reporting this because there is no way this was an owl. It stood upright like a man, just really, really tall. I don't want to discuss this with anyone and would prefer to remain anonymous. I don't imagine anyone would believe me anyway. One of the guys I work with, who saw this thing, said that it made him feel very uneasy, like a scared kid. He was glad someone threw a rock and made it fly away."

Since this report was sent to MUFON, I had no way of knowing the identity of the witness. There was a later attempt by MUFON to interview the witness (from information that I received from a field investigator), but the witness was never located. I will state that I was contacted by an official at MUFON, after a few more sightings were reported to the Case Management System. The official, who said that the organization would 'like to mutually share information' in an attempt to interview witnesses, later discounted the sightings as merely misidentified birds or people in winged suits. Needless to say, any further cooperation with MUFON was out of the question.

A FEW DAYS LATER, another report was forwarded to MUFON:

Chicago, IL - 2017-04-16: "I was hanging out with my boys and a few friends. As we talked about work and our families we heard what sounded like a bird flapping its wings. One of my homies yelled out that he saw a huge 'Lechuza' (Spanish for 'Barn Owl') over by the road. We walked over there and saw what look like a big owl. As we walked up on it this owl, it stood up on two feet and looked right at us. We saw what look like a huge Lechuza, except it was about six feet tall and really big. It had large glowing red eyes that were completely freaking everybody out. We all yelled and this thing took off into the air and flew towards North Ave. This thing freaked us all out and scared all our kids." Once again, we had no witness contact information since this account was forwarded to the MUFON CMS.

A 'Lechuza' or La Lechuza, which the witness identified the being as, is a legendary witch that can transform itself into a large owl-like being. In most accounts, the face of transformed being remains as that of the witch. The supposed winged being is said to swoop down and attack its victims, as well as loudly screeching; similar to the sound made by a Banshee. I have been told that this tradition is well-known in Hispanic cultures located just north and south of the Rio Grande Valley.

This was a second reference to an owl-like winged being. Though the reports were not very detailed, and that we were unable to conduct an interview, I believe that there was legitimacy in the witness statements. The information about a winged being in the Chicago area had only been reported by MUFON, Phantoms & Monsters and UFO Clearinghouse. None of the local media was reporting any of these accounts and, frankly, the paranormal and cryptozoology communities weren't focused on the reports either.

ON THE SAME day that the 'Lechuza' report was post to the MUFON CMS, another account surfaced. This time, a bat-like winged being seen flying off-shore on Lake Michigan:

"*Chicago, IL - 2017-04-15: I was out on the lake with my husband and two other couples celebrating a friend's birthday. We were about two miles out on the lake, just off of Montrose Beach at about 10pm. We were enjoying ourselves when I happened to look up and saw what looked like a giant bat (and not like a Flying Fox which I looked up and saw was the biggest bat). This bat was as tall as my husband, who is six foot four inches or even bigger. It was solid black with eyes that seemed to reflect the moonlight. This bat was blacker than the surrounding night and was perfectly silhouetted against the moonlit sky. This bat circled the boat three times in complete silence before heading off towards Montrose. It quickly blended into the night sky and was gone in seconds.*

About five minutes after seeing this bat we saw a bright green object traveling north to south at the horizon. It was not a plane as it was brilliant green and was moving slowly across the horizon. If I had to estimate, it was about two miles from our position.

After the object was out of sight, we sat there looking around in stunned silence. I began feeling this overwhelming sensation of dread and told my husband that I felt that it was prudent that we get off the water as quickly as possible. I tried to get a picture of the thing as it circled our boat, but all I got was black."

At that point, I was beginning to wonder if we were dealing with two separate winged beings. It also appeared that whatever this was, it allowed itself to be seen; but only giving the witnesses enough time to get a fleeting glance before it quickly flew away.

But one factor had become obvious to me. These four sightings had been made within an eight day period; and no other closely reported group of flying humanoid sightings had been known to exist since the 1966-67 Mothman accounts from Point Pleasant, WV. Little did we know this was only the 'tip of the iceberg.'

4

'BAT OUT OF HELL'

AFTER A LULL of approximately two weeks, a witness report was forwarded to UFO Clearinghouse on April 30, 2017. A father and son, who were fishing in the Little Calumet River, were startled by a large flying anomaly:

> "On Thursday, April 27, 2017, I was out with my son by the banks of the Little Calumet River, on the northwest side off of Hegewisch Marsh Park at a spot where we have had some success catching fish in the past. It's located by the trestle bridge that runs east to west over near 130th Street. It's a spot that takes a little effort to get to, but it has had some payoffs in catching some medium-sized catfish.
>
> It was about 7:30pm and we were packing up our gear when we heard something that sounded like train brakes when the train is slowing down. The problem was there was no train going by at the moment. When the train goes by, you usually feel it. You also hear it as it's pretty loud. On this day, it was quiet with the occasional sound of trucks or cars going about. We heard the sound again and saw something fly from our left

toward some trees on the other side of the river. We thought it looked like a giant bird, but it was solid black.

Within a minute, we heard the sound again and this thing flew straight up and over the trestle bridge and headed off down the river. This thing was unlike any bird we have seen in our lives. It was solid black and had to be about the size of a full grown man. It had wings that must have been ten feet from tip to tip. It flew up and out of sight within seconds. We couldn't really get many details, as this thing flew like a literal 'bat out of hell' and was still on the other side of the river. We stood there and watched it fly away. I was just blown away.

But then my son piped up and said he had read about some giant bat sightings that have occurred in Chicago lately; maybe this was one of them. We packed up our gear and got the hell out of there as fast as we could. We didn't want this thing to come back and see us there as we were not supposed to be there fishing in the first place.

Later that night my son showed me the websites where the reports were listed and that lead me to report this sighting. I'm sorry that I couldn't give you more details on this thing, but frankly, I thank my lucky stars that we weren't close enough to see any details."

ABOUT A WEEK later Manuel received an email, then a follow-up telephone call, from a witness; who happened to be an Illinois State Trooper.

Manuel stated that he was contacted on the evening of Sunday, May 7, 2017, in regard to a sighting on Friday, May 5, 2017, at about 8 pm in the area around Calumet Park in the far south side of the city near the Indiana border. The witness described a large bat-like creature flying at great speed over the park and toward the field house that is located in the center of the park. I spoke with the witness, who described himself as a law enforcement officer, concerning the incident. The witness was accompanied by his ten year-old son and was out walking the footpaths of the park.

Calumet Park is a lakeside park located in the South Chicago/Calumet Park neighborhood that is popular with bikers, joggers and roller skaters and offers a wide variety of activities throughout the spring and summer. It is a popular spot for many people that live in the southern portion of the city and a popular beach during the summer months. Here's the original email:

"I was out with my son at Calumet Park at about 8pm walking the trail, as we have since he was about six years old. We were talking about what was going on in our lives and about what our plans were for the upcoming summer. As we walked toward the field house, we were over flown by what I thought was a large goose, as we have seen multiple geese flying around the city and suburbs within the last couple of months. As we watched, it quickly became apparent that this was not a goose, but something much bigger.

I can describe it as a large bat, but it had a distinct human figure about six feet in height per my estimate. It was black/gray in color and had an enormous pair of wings that must have been eight to ten feet in width. My son was in complete shock and asked me what that thing was. My response was an equally surprised "I don't know." This bat flew up and over the field house and toward the tennis courts. I heard a couple yell out in surprise as this bat flew up and over the field house and out of view. The entire encounter lasted about thirty to thirty-five seconds from the initial sighting, to it flying up and over the field house and out of sight.

I estimate the speed of this bat to be at least forty to fifty miles per hour and it to be at least fifteen to twenty feet above us as it was just over the top of the streetlights. It was dusk, but the sun had just started to set, so there was enough light to still get a good view of the object as it flew overhead. I was only able to get a general description as it flew over us at that speed and prohibited from getting any finer detail of it. We went around the field house in an attempt to see anything on the other side, but did not get any other views of this creature. The rest of the evening went without incident and I only decided to report this after reading some reports of similar sightings within the city online."

By the time that this report reached Manuel, the 'buzz' was starting to circulate among the citizens of Chicago. I began to post my contact information on local internet boards and other social media. It was important that people were not afraid or wary about reporting this phenomenon. I wanted the witnesses to know upfront that any information that they provided to me would be posted in the strictest confidence. This has been my policy since I started blogging on Phantoms & Monsters.

THEN A REPORT REACHED the MUFON CMS that even surprised me. A pair of winged beings had been seen flying together over a downtown marina:

Chicago, IL - 2017-05-19: "I was out at the breakwater with my best friend and her boyfriend. We were waiting for my boyfriend to finish helping his dad tie their boat to the dock after helping bring the boat to the marina for the summer.

We were standing on the shore by some picnic tables

waiting on James to meet us there. We were talking when we heard this loud screech. It sounded completely out of this world and after a couple of seconds, we heard another one, only louder and higher pitch than the first one. We looked around thinking we had heard an animal in distress and wondered if it needed help. That's when we saw this large bat fly into our view.

It was black and came from the direction of the bridge that holds up Lake Shore Drive. It flew low and then shot up into the air as it came over the water. We noticed one of the coast guard helicopters was flying over the water at about the same time, but we're not sure if it saw this thing as it kept on flying toward the Adler Planetarium.

This thing flew a large circle and cried out again. Almost instantly it was joined by another large bat. These things were big and stood out against the sky. They flew figure eights around each other. It looked like they were dancing in a strange sort of way. It was actually quite beautiful, considering how freaking strange it was.

About that time, my boyfriend walked up on us and scared the living bejesus out of us. Both myself and my friend screamed and I think those large bats heard us, because they screeched back at each other and both flew down toward the water. It looked like they were going to slam into the water and at the last second, they pulled up and flew toward and under the bridge; and out of sight. We ran toward the railing, to look down the river and saw nothing else.

This entire encounter lasted about one and a half to two minutes. It was scary, only because we didn't know what the Hell they were, but it looked like they were interested in each other and not us. We can't be the only other ones to see it. The river walk and the pier were full of people and joggers. Are these things just giant bats or are they gargoyles?

This is the first account, that I can ever recall, where two winged humanoids were seen flying together; let alone performing difficult maneuvers.

This incident occurred in an area where literally hundreds of people had congregated. Were we going to receive more reports? Maybe someone had time to get a photograph?

THEN MANUEL RECEIVED an email from another witness, who had been on the river walk on the same day (5/19/2017 – approx. 8PM) as the downtown marina sighting:

"I was out with my daughter and mother celebrating my daughter's recent graduation. After dinner and some light shopping, we decided to go out and check out the newly opened Chicago River Walk that had just opened after construction. We accessed the river walk via the entrance on Michigan Avenue and walked east toward the lake, looking at the sights and enjoying the beautiful view.

As we passed under the Columbus Drive Bridge, we heard this strange sound and my daughter said, "Look at that!" As we looked up, we saw a large winged "person" flying just above the water and then pulling up and going OVER the bridge! It looked like a huge owl or even a bat, but completely black with the exception of the two large eyes that appeared red. I'm not sure if it was the actual color of its eyes or just the light reflecting off of them, either way it looked very spooky.

We watched it go over the bridge and then continue flying right above the water and out of sight. It didn't seem to care if anyone else saw it; just flying above the water until it was out of sight. My daughter and I tried to get pictures of it, but all we got were blurry images of mostly black. My daughter did sketch what she saw and I have included it in this email.

We have never seen anything like this before. It never flapped its wings while we were in sight. At first glance, it looked like a person in a wing suit, but I don't think anyone would be suicidal enough to go for a stunt like that along the waterfront.

I have gone skydiving before and have seen demonstrations of wing suits in the past. This lead me to rule out that this would be a person in one of those suits or anything similar as it would be a sure-fire recipe for disaster.

This thing also had wings that did seem a bit like the wings on a bat. It formed one big wing from the back to the bottom of the legs and seemed more of a membrane, than feathered wings like an owl. There was no sound at all, just an audible whoosh as it flew over. It was up and over the bridge in a matter of seconds and then it was gone. We were a bit shaken up after this thing flew away. We didn't know what it was that we had seen."

Manuel was able to interview the witnesses later on, though there was no further information. They didn't embellish on their original email, and were quite confident that what they witnessed was a living being, and not a drone or person in a wing suit.

We had been hoping that there would be photographs available, but by this time some of the witnesses were telling us that the photographs were nothing but black splotches or totally blacked out.

Not long after I had posted this account, a number of naysayers suddenly came out of the woodwork. It was a litany of the typical responses. Maybe it was a large, possibly mutated, Sand Hill Crane or a disguised drone? Maybe the city was involved in a promotion or viral campaign to beef up tourism by using a person in a squirrel suit? As absurd some of these suggestions were, there was a clear intention to tap down any significance of the sightings.

It became apparent, not long after the downtown sightings began, that the Chicago City government or the Chicago Police Department wanted nothing to do with the reports. Our team, who I called the 'Chicago Phantom Task Force,' made numerous FOIA requests that were quickly dismissed. I'll get into that aspect of these sightings later on.

Witness's rendering of the downtown winged being.

ON SUNDAY, May 27, 2017, I received a telephone call from a witness in the Calumet Park neighborhood of Chicago. Here is the report:

> A woman and her boyfriend noticed a large black figure hovering above a group of trees in the vicinity of 127th and Ashland Ave. at approximately 7:30 PM on Saturday, May 27. The witnesses state that they first thought that it was a black helicopter because of the size, though the distance was not determined. The object then rose further in the sky and became apparent that it was a large human-like being with wings.
>
> They described it as black in color and that it was flying without moving its wings. They were shocked at the size as it silhouetted itself across the moon, which was visible in the late clear evening. There was still considerable light, but too dark to get a discernible video or photograph with their cell phone, though there was an attempt to capture photographic evidence.
>
> They determined that it was not a plane or glider, but a living being of unknown origin. The description by the woman was that is looked like a 'large black flying man with wings.'
>
> The woman (who did disclose her name to me) was disturbed by this encounter. She searched the internet and discovered my posts on Phantoms & Monsters. She was surprised by the previous sightings in Chicago; which she was not aware of. She plans to be vigilant during the next few evenings and will be making inquiries of possible sightings by other witnesses.

I found that the witnesses were very credible and made no attempt to embellish their sighting.

I believed that it was time to give these flying humanoids an exclusive moniker, so that there would a distinction between these sightings and the Mothman. I started to refer to this winged being as the 'Chicago Phantom.'

By the time I received this report, I had been made aware of a series of bright white flashes of light occurring in various areas south of the city. There had been two reports from the Chicago Heights area and another just across the Indiana line near Hammond, IN.

Over the years, there has been some speculation in the paranormal community that there may be a connection with bright flashes of light and orb activity in areas where cryptid sightings had been reported. Several Bigfoot investigators have made me aware that while they would be examining an encounter or sighting location, they would notice visible white orbs moving about. There have also been accounts of bright flashes of light in regions where known Bigfoot activity has been reported.

Pennsylvania UFO and anomalies researcher Stan Gordon has also reported the presence of UFO and Bigfoot activity in tandem over the past two decades that he has been investigating the phenomenon. Reports of bright flashes of light have been theorized to be associated with the opening of inter-dimensional portals or wormholes. It is a theory that I believe may somehow offer insight as to why various cryptids or entities seem to have an ability to suddenly vanish from certain locations. Can this theory be applied to the Chicago Phantom sightings? That remains to be seen.

5

AN EARLIER SIGHTING SURFACES

I RECEIVED an email on evening of Sunday May 28, 2017, from another flying humanoid witness in Chicago. His name is Billy Bantz, and he wanted to talk to me. His sighting, at this time, is the earliest in 2017. The following account was his initial contact by email:

> *"My name is Billy Bantz. I drive a semi with a large carrier company in Chicago. On March 22, I was at a delivery location at Cicero Ave. and 290 Expressway in Chicago. I was picking up a load of bread there. I noticed a flying object at around noon in the airspace to the south coming from Midway Airport. The object looked like a man with wings; like Batman. I thought it was an experimental drone or secret government military test. After seeing the picture by the Indian statue (8/22/2011, 63rd and Pulaski Rd in Chicago, IL sighting), I am convinced it was the thing these other folks have seen.*
>
> *I have three witnesses for that day and the text to prove it happened. I absolutely swear it was this "Mothman." The object was gliding over me and disappeared in the clouds. It is*

very loud by the expressway and I have had no recollection of screaming. Shortly after I saw this thing, I had a litany of strange health problems that are documented. My eyes are even messed up, like the movie and other claims. I have all the documentation to prove my story.

I hope I am not considered a freak after this but this sighting can be proven well before the other sightings were reported. I have nothing to gain by reporting this, so call me if you have questions. The health issues are very odd and serious. I have had several MRI tests and a lumbar puncture due to the pressure behind my eyes."

Billy Bantz' rendering of the flying being.

I called Billy as soon as I received the email. He explained that this figure was the size of a large automobile, and looked exactly like the 8/22/2011 sighting photo. He also mentioned that it was in Midway International Airport airspace.

Billy also forwarded documentation proving the bizarre medical problems he has endured since the sighting; eventually traced to an extremely rare condition in his eyes. As well, he forwarded documentation on his mother's death, which occurred unexpectedly approximately three weeks ago. I have no proof that these incidents are related to the sighting, but it is noteworthy nonetheless and part of the record.

Billy was very forthcoming and answered all my questions without embellishment. I truly believe he witnessed what he described, which he believes was a winged living being.

Over the months, Billy has kept in touch with me and has also made himself willingly available to colleagues who are interested in the Chicago Phantom sightings. His contribution to our investigation has been noteworthy and appreciated.

———

I RECEIVED a telephone call at 12:04 AM ET (Sunday, June 4, 2017) from a witness who stated that her and her boyfriend saw a "large man with bat wings" in the 400 block of N. Arlington Place (between N. Clark St. and N. Lakeview Ave.) in the Lincoln Park community of Chicago.

> *"The couple called me from the location after the encounter. It took them about an hour to search Google for similar sightings and to find my telephone number. The sighting was on Saturday 6/3/2017 at approximately 10PM CT local time.*
>
> *Both witnesses talked to me. They were both shook up and assured me that neither of them drink alcohol or take drugs.*

Both are professionals and business owners in the Chicago area. They had just finished a late dinner at a local restaurant and noticed the flying anomaly as they were walking on the 400 block of N. Arlington Place. The street lights illuminated the figure enough to startle them, so it could not have been very high above the street.

They both described it as a seven to eight foot solid black humanoid with wide membrane wings that resembled those of a huge bat. The wing span was at least twelve feet The head was prominent, and thinner than a human head. The back end of the body tampered to a point. No legs were noticed, but could have been tucked up under the body. The figure was gliding quickly along the length of the street heading east, then suddenly ascended into the night sky. Neither heard any sound. Both witnesses told me that they felt a sense of foreboding and were still terrified almost an hour after the encounter."

The fear in their voices was palpable. I actually felt sorry that they had witnessed something that scared them so badly.

THEN UFO CLEARINGHOUSE received a report from another witness who had seen the same winged being, at the same location and at the same time:

"I was walking with my boyfriend in Lincoln Park around 10PM tonight on Saturday, June 3, and saw a huge bat or what I could only describe as a bat glide past. It was huge and long. I can't explain what it was but it was not normal. It was pitch black and had no feathers. I thought it was an eagle or a bat, but it was definitely bigger than both of those. Its wings were *skin-like and it made no sound. I called my boyfriend to see it but by the time he looked he only saw the tail end of it.*

We both felt very uneasy and more uneasy after Googling and coming across similar reports. I'm not sure what to make of it but it was not normal. The wings were longer than my boyfriends' arms and he's six feet."

This report was the first to describe a thin head that seemed to be pointed in shape. Later sightings offered more details as to the shape of the head and a possible crest like structure extending the top.

———

THESE TWO SIGHTINGS in Lincoln Park were only a few blocks from the Oz Park encounter. There would another report only a few blocks north of this location, that was sent to Manuel about a month after the sighting. After the Lincoln Park sightings, we didn't receive a report for about two weeks, though we later found out that the Phantom had been busy; but witnesses were hesitant to report what they had seen. Then a report was received by UFO Clearinghouse:

"I was out for a late jog on Saturday evening about 7PM, June 17, 2017, and was taking my usual route along the lakefront jogging trail headed toward the Navy Pier. As I passed Ohio Street Beach and headed toward the Pier, I saw what looked like a giant bat fly over from what looked like under the bridge that holds up North Lakeshore Drive. It flew parallel to East Grand Avenue and then up and over the trees toward the water treatment plant. The whole incident only lasted a few seconds and getting any exact details was hard due to the low light. I can make an educated guess and say that it looked like

it was the height of an average man at about six foot tall, but I also was maybe fifteen to twenty feet away from it when I saw it.

It looked like a great big bat, solid black but it stood out against the building and had a wingspan that must have been at least seven to eight feet from tip to tip. It was silent as far as I could tell but there was a lot of city noise in that area with traffic and what not. I know I was not the only one who saw it as about six to seven others noticed it and I heard more than one person say, "Look at that!" As it flew, you could tell it was flapping its large wings; gaining speed and altitude till it cleared the trees and headed off toward the water treatment plant. When I reached the point where I could look out toward the plant, it was gone.

I checked my watch at that time and noted the time was 7:08 pm and the weather was cloudy. We had storms pass through the area earlier today and it looked like more were on the way. There was visible lightning over the lake at the time that this incident occurred. I went home after my jog was completed and looked up sightings of giant bats in the city and was shocked by how many there were recently. That is how I got the info on where to report my sighting"

Once again, an overpass or bridge on North Lakeshore Drive was mentioned as a possible location as to where this being was coming or going. The Task Force discussed if there was a possibility that a physical entrance to an underground tunnel or facility could be accessed from under one of these overpass locations. It seems that there is a vast underground system that runs along the lake shore; but access is limited only to authorized personnel.

I also received an unsubstantiated report of a flying being seen high above the United Center from a witness on W.

Monroe St. This information was told to me by telephone, by a MUFON field investigator who assured me that they would be interviewing the witness and that they would get back to me. I never heard another word about this supposed sighting, no surprise there.

6

'IT WAS NOT OF THIS WORLD'

I HAD MENTIONED EARLIER that there was a sighting in which the witnesses waited about a month before they reported it. The sighting took place on May 27, 2017, and was forwarded to UFO Clearinghouse:

> "I would like to tell you about an incident that happened on Saturday, May 27, 2017, near our home in Chicago. We were returning home after going out to dinner with some friends at a neighborhood Thai food restaurant. The time was about 10:30ish at night and we were walking hand-in-hand toward home. As we approach the intersection of Wrightwood and Lakeview (N. Wrightwood Ave and N. Lakeview Ave.) my husband noticed something flying above us headed toward the west. It was flying approximately fifteen feet in the air and moving along at brisk pace. It looked like a giant bat only it was way larger and solid black.
>
> The object would have been almost solid black if it were not for 2 glowing red eyes staring back at us. It flew overhead, circled back and flew over us again before heading back toward the park. This object was far larger than anything I

have ever seen in and around the park or the lakefront. I've seen large birds in the area but could recognize them as birds and nothing grew even close to the size this thing was. My husband said that whatever it was 'was not of this world' and 'if it was, it was undiscovered,' but he was absolutely speechless and could not provide an explanation to what we saw.

We discussed it all the way home and afterwards I did some searching on the internet for a possible explanation when I ran across reported sightings, some of them very close to our neighborhood. I showed them to my husband who still remains skeptical and said that we should not report what we saw. He stated that no one would believe that we saw a huge man-bat flying over Chicago and that people would possibly laugh at us.

I reported it because I want to have an explanation to what we saw that night. Neither one of us are crazy and we both saw exactly the same thing. We just want to have an explanation as to what we saw that night. My husband said he wanted to just put it behind him but if I wanted to report it, then I was more than welcome to; so that's what I did. Perhaps somebody can provide a perfectly logical explanation of what we saw in the night sky. Thank you for your time and attention and I hope to hear from you soon."

It was now apparent that at least one of these winged beings preferred North Lake Shore Drive and the neighborhoods in the vicinity.

By this time, I was receiving interview requests from local drive-time radio shows and several online paranormal programs. People were beginning to ask questions. They wanted to know what was being seen in their city and, more importantly, what these sightings meant. Was it a harbinger of some type? I tried to dispel any notion that Chicago had a disaster in its future. But the internet bloggers were comparing these sightings to the Mothman, and the theory that its presence was a warning that the Silver Bridge would soon collapse over the Ohio River.

There were psychics from all over the country calling and giving me their 'visions' of Chicago's future. Some people had read where I had predicted, and posted at the beginning of 2017, that I sensed there would be a major bridge disaster in the United States. I'll admit it, I did post that statement, but I never mentioned a location and I never felt that Chicago was in the crosshairs.

A FEW DAYS after the Navy Pier encounter, UFO Clearinghouse received a report from a witness who had been with a group of friends while visiting the Adler Planetarium:

"I want to tell you about a sighting that happened on Friday the 23rd of June at about 9:30 p.m. by the Adler Planetarium in Chicago, Illinois. My girlfriend and I are spending the weekend in Chicago and we took a walk around the Adler and Shedd Aquarium so she could try to get some more Pokemon. We were spending our anniversary together downtown and wanted to visit the museum campus. We were at the backside of the Adler Planetarium and had walked along the path toward the food court.

We ordered some food and sat down when there was commotion and a bunch of people were shouting and pointing at the sky. We both got up and went to look what was going on and saw a large black bat like creature headed away from us. When we asked people what they had seen we were told that they had seen a large bat. Everyone described it as a large bat like creature that also had human-like features.

Rendition of Wrightwood-Lakeview sighting by Emily Wayland.

What we saw was flying away from us but supported what everyone else has seen as looking like a large bat. We hung around for about 30 minutes after that looking up at the sky, as was everybody else. No one saw or heard anything for the remainder of time that we were there. There was the feeling of uneasiness amongst the people who were there and many shortly departed right before we did."

APPROXIMATELY A WEEK LATER, I received the following report on Sunday, July 2, at 3:00PM ET:

"Good afternoon, I wanted to write in and report a sighting that happened to me and my two friends a few weeks ago along the lake shore of Chicago.

We decided to report this after reading your blog about a similar sighting that happened the same night of ours. The events that I'm writing about happened on Friday, June 23,

2017, at approximately 10PM I was with a group of friends at the Adler Planetarium just hanging out and having fun down by the concession area. We usually hang out at the lake side because it's fun and you get to meet a lot of girls. This particular night we were hanging out at our usual table near the taco stand when we saw what had to be the biggest bat we have ever seen. This bat must have been at least seven feet tall if he was standing up but again, my perception might be skewed because it was dark and this thing was about twenty feet up in the air. All three of us were like; "What the f*** is that?!"

We all saw it about the same time as it flew over and continued toward the area of Soldier Field. It did this for maybe 20 yards or so, then abruptly changed directions and headed toward the lake and flew out over the lake and out of sight. This thing made no noise and was easily seen by myself and at least a few other people. We were so preoccupied with looking at this flying thing that none of us thought about grabbing our phones and taking pictures.

My friend sent me an email with a link about a similar sighting in the same general area on the same night we had ours. That is why I am writing to report our sighting that we had that night. I am more than willing to talk about the sighting as long as my name is not used and my friends who were with me that night are too.

Thank you for taking my report and not thinking I am crazy because of what we saw. The one thing that does not fit in with the similar sighting that I saw on your site is there was no feeling of dread or despair, but an overwhelming urge to keep a looking at the creature. But that could have also been morbid curiosity. - TA."

After talking to this witness, I was starting to sense that this being was attempting to communicate to a wider audience without exposing itself excessively.

In fact, the witness relayed a bucolic-like experience, even though he and his companions were surprised by the encounter. This seemed to be the overall attitude by the multitude of witness outside the Adler Planetarium that particular evening. Once again, the witnesses were not inclined to take photographs.

The inability of the witnesses to secure a photograph, even when there is an opportunity, has caused considerable discussion among our team and others. One theory is that the witnesses are somehow 'paralyzed' with surprise or shock during the sighting, which is plausible considering what people are reporting. Another theory is that the being itself is controlling the response of the witnesses, rendering them unable to react. This premise may have some substance to it. It has been said that some cryptids may possess an ESP-like capacity that can be used to communicate with human witnesses.

A large number of Bigfoot experiencers have reported a similar phenomenon. Some of the Mothman and other flying humanoid testimonials have mentioned confusion and receiving hypnotic messages. I suppose the debate will continue until a discernible photograph or video is obtained.

ON JULY 5, 2017, I received a brief email from a lounge bouncer who mentioned that he had a run-in with, what he called, a 'flying bat-like humanoid.' He also mentioned that he would like to talk to me, since he also had questions about the being he had witnessed. After the witness and I talked, I posted the following information:

"I recently received an email from a witness in Chicago, who stated that they wished to talk to me about a sighting he had on Friday, June 30, at approximately 10:30PM. The witness works security at a bar named; 'The Owl' located in the 2500 block of N. Milwaukee Ave in Logan Square.

The witness states that he was outside the location, leaning against the wall while smoking a cigarette. He was alone at the time, except a few other people walking along the street. He noticed a large 'bat-like' creature flying above the street lights (approximately seventy to eighty feet away) over the lot across the street. As the witness focused on the flying anomaly, he noticed that it was actually a bat-like humanoid. The body was five to five and a half feet in length and grayish in color (it was well-illuminated by the street lights). The head was human-like, but was much thinner and had a pointed crest extending from the back of its head (similar to a pterosaur, but shorter). The head was turned away from the witness, so he could not see the eyes or face.

The body tapered towards the back and it looked like there were short legs or appendages tucked underneath it, followed by a short rounded extension or tail. The wings had a full span of approximately eight to ten feet and were attached along the body. The wings were a bat-like membrane, but heavy like that of a pterosaur. The witness noticed that the being flapped its wings to gain speed and height, then would glide. There was no sound. It was moving swiftly above the street lights across N. Milwaukee Ave., then burst upwards into the clouds. He was not sure if there were other witnesses, since the being flew by quickly. The witness said that at the time, his phone was inside the bar charging; and that he was very upset he didn't have it because he would have had time to get a photograph. He said that he didn't feel any fear or foreboding, only that he was startled at what he witnessed. The witness was very *convincing, forthright and did not embellish during his account."*

This was the first witness to state that there was a crest structure extending from the top of the head towards the back. A previous account mentioned a pointed head, but not an extended crest.

This was also the point where I was confident that people were seeing multiple winged beings. I was more convinced of this theory when the sightings started to regularly reach into the suburbs and beyond. The description differences were part of my concept process, but there was also the fact that the locations and times of the sightings were so sporadic.

The Task Force continued to attempt to formulate a pattern with the sightings and witnesses, but the hap-hazard modus suggested to me that there may be multiple beings moving between worlds or realities. A lot of people thought I was going off the deep end when I started to float the idea of inter-dimensional beings. But if I've learned one thing after 40 years of investigating the unknown; it's that you should be open-minded and that nothing should surprise you.

7

'CHICAGO'S FINEST' MEET THE 'CHICAGO PHANTOM'

UFO CLEARINGHOUSE RECEIVED a narrative from a Chicago police officer in reference to an encounter he and his partner had two weeks prior. I'll be the first to admit, I was a bit skeptical when I was told by Manuel that a patrol officer came forward with an account. But I was convinced of his story after reading it and looking at the location.

Here is the report:

"I'm going to tell you about something that happened to me on the night of June 29, 2017, in Chicago, Illinois. I am reporting this of my own volition and I want to stay anonymous due to the fact that I work for the Chicago Police Department and do not want anybody else to know that I submitted this report. I have been with the Chicago Police Department for over eight and a half years.

The only people who know that I submitted this are my wife, my son who encouraged me to submit this and my partner who also was witness to this incident. I want you to know that I am of a sound mind and health and I don't want any publicity other than just reporting this incident. I also want you to know that I am not prone to fits of fantasy or hoaxing anything that I've seen; especially while I am on duty.

On the night of June 29, 2017, at approximately 11:15 p.m. my partner and I were on routine patrol and approaching the intersection of West 81st and South Throop in the Auburn Gresham neighborhood of Chicago, Illinois. We were flagged down by a group of a people who were pointing up to the top of an apartment building that was on the corner. We pulled over and they immediately started telling us to look up at the building. Many of the people were very frightened and were very excited about seeing what they had seen.

My partner and I look and see a large creature that was approximately six to six and a half feet tall and was very thin. If it had been a human it would have been emaciated. This thing was standing on top of the building and had what looked like a pair of very large wings that extended out at least eight to ten feet from tip-to-tip. No discernible features, it just looked like a dark black shadow with wings. My partner and I both thought it was somebody trying to jump from the building and maybe wearing a costume of some kind. When we both shined our flashlights to try to get a better look at what we were dealing with, this thing took off into the air and flew away.

As this creature flew away, headed in a southern direction, something sounding like a scream came from it and within the matter of about five-seconds this creature was gone into the night. The people who initially flagged us down had said that many people in the neighborhood had seen this thing for the previous two nights and this just happened to be the only time that it was seen in a stationary place. We stood there stunned as this thing flew away and disappeared into the night. We stood there and talked to the group of people who flagged us down, taking information down and any information regarding previous sightings from the nights before. We *initially were doubtful about filing a report because we thought we would be made fun of for seeing Little Green Men. We finally filed a report as we did not want to violate protocol. Nothing was ever said about the report being filed and as of right now it's been business as usual.*

We wanted to file this report because after I told my son the story, he went online and showed me that this is not the only sighting of something similar being seen in the city. I showed my partner the day after the sighting and he said that he didn't want to be involved and as far as he was concerned it was nothing more than a large owl or big bird that was misidentified. My son was the one who encouraged me to file this and do it anonymously to protect my identity.

I know what I saw was real and even though I have no explanation as to what it truly is, I know that what I saw was flesh and blood. I am a Christian man who believes that there are things that come from other planes and stalk the people of this Earth and that only one's faith is what protects us from these things. I know that my faith is strong and therefore I am protected and I hope that I never see this thing again. Thank you very much for your time and have a blessed day."

Any man or woman who enjoys a strong faith in whatever or whoever they believe in, and patrols the mean streets of Chicago with the confidence of their convictions, deserves my trust in what they say. The Task Force, in unison, commented that a FOIA application needed to be filed with the Chicago Police Department. The application was filed; and responded to within a few days. The Chicago Police Department had 'no record' of a report. Well, first of all, a FOIA application is never responded to in just a few days. I don't care what department at any branch of government in these United States receives it. It was obvious to us that this application had been flagged and taken care of as soon as possible. There were three more FOIA applications filed with the CPD; and all three were responded to within a few days and with the same response.

By that time, I had been talking to a few Chicago municipal workers, as well as an associate who worked at City Hall. People within the city government were aware of the sightings, and for some unknown reason they were determined not to acknowledge it. Were the powers that be afraid it would cause a panic? Would it interfere with the summer tourist season? Or did they just want one less uneasy subject to deal with; along with the high murder rate and fiscal disaster already in their midst?

ANYWAY; approximately a month after the police officer's incident in Auburn Gresham and two weeks after the report was sent to Manuel, I received a follow-up from one of the citizen witnesses at the scene:

"Mr. Strickler, I hesitated to send this in for two reasons: first, I'm still not one hundred percent sure that I believe it myself, and second, I'm trying to be a journalist and I don't want this kind of a report to discredit me for future career opportunities. That's why I'm sending this anonymously, and that's why I'm not interested in following up about any of this.

I was talking about this story while drinking with my siblings the other night and my sister pointed out that it reminded her of some stories she'd seen circulating online.

When I looked into it myself, I was surprised to see that my story had already been partially reported earlier this month. On June 29, I was walking home from getting Wendy's with a small group of friends when one of my friends pointed at a dark shape in a tree on the corner of West 81st and South

Throop. The thing was big, but details were hard to make out at night.

Then the thing jumped out of the tree and flew onto the roof of an apartment building on the same block.

When it flew, I got the chance to see that it was a tall dark thing with wide wings. Nothing like that Mothman statue they've got in Point Pleasant. A group of people had started to form on the corner with my friends and me.

Then some of the people on the corner whom I hadn't met previously flagged down a cop car to point the thing out. That's when my friends and I quietly slipped away. I'm a transgender woman and I've had my share of bad interactions with the police. My friends felt similarly.

I now believe that the officer I saw was the same officer who reported a story about seeing this thing on the same night.

I still think it might have had a logical explanation, but I thought there might be others interested in hearing this story and coming to their own conclusions. Thank you."

I was very heartened that this witness came forward to substantiate the police officer's statements and to add to the account.

There has been an aspect to the witnesses of this phenomenon that I want to point out. These people are just ordinary members of society, whether you agree or disagree with their lifestyle or retain any other form of prejudice towards them. They have all seen the same thing, and have experienced the same shock or disbelief. But they also took the time and effort to contact someone with their account.

When I mention in the blog or on a radio show that the witnesses have been remarkably forthright and have refused to embellish on their original testimony, it comes from a researcher who has talked to literally thousands of witnesses over many years. The people who have contacted me concerning this winged being in the Chicago metro area have been some the best observers I have ever dealt with. There was a period of about four weeks in July 2017, in which no new reports were received. In fact, several of us on the Task Force were thinking aloud that this flap of sightings may be coming to an end.

BUT THEN I received a telephone call from the witness (Guillermo) at 7:38PM ET on Monday, July 24, 2017, who stated that he witnessed a flying human-like being at approximately 5:10PM CT that same day. This was a time difference of 1 hour 18 mins between the sighting and the call.

The witness states that he was outside the Franklin Tap on 325 S. Franklin St. while smoking a cigarette. He was alone at the time, though there were many people walking along the sidewalk. He happened to look up towards the Willis Tower, located at 233 S. Wacker Drive, and noticed a human-like figure standing near the top of the building. In a perched position, the being looked like a six foot human with tall wings that extended a few feet above the body. As he watched, the being leaped off the building, stretched out the wings, dipped and swooped upwards. It gained altitude as it flapped its wings and headed off in a northern direction.

The witness states that the being's outstretched wings were not very large, maybe six to eight feet from tip-tip, but were very jagged and insect-like (shaped similar to a moth). The being was also dark green in color and had a body form like that of a mantis. The legs seemed to be human-like and extended beyond the body while flying. He called it a; "human, insect and bird mix" that seemed to mutate while in flight.

The witness tells me that he had not heard of any of the

previous sightings, and that other people he talked to were unaware of the sightings as well. I asked the witness to stay in touch; I have his contact information.

Guillermo told me that immediately after the incident, he was attempting to calm down and then find somewhere to report this sighting. He found my telephone number online and then called. He still seemed somewhat distressed when we talked.

His description was different from the previous accounts, especially the mantis-like body, insect-like wings and dark green in color. He also stated that it 'mutated' in mid-flight. I assume he meant that it changed in form. Since he observed this being at such a great distance, his descriptions may have been skewed somewhat. I'm not saying that I don't believe the information, but it remains ambiguous.

———

UFO CLEARINGHOUSE RECEIVED the following report at the end of July 2017:

> *"Hi, I saw that you were keeping a timeline of; "batman" sightings in Chicago. My friend and I just saw something in Albany Park/Lincoln Square, about half an hour ago (7/29 - 10:30PM CT), and I'm not sure who to report it to.*
>
> *It was a huge black shape that appeared to be gliding high over the Wilson/Kimball area. We viewed it from my balcony about half a mile north of there. We observed it gliding for about two minutes before it was lost in the clouds, headed south. It looked somewhat like a bat and that's what I thought it was at first, but it was just too big! It was hard to tell exactly how big from that distance, but I would guess about an eight foot wingspan.*

We're pretty spooked by it. Let me know if you have any advice about who we should report this to. Thanks, AJ."

I don't believe the witnesses provided a following up interview, though there was a very grainy video that showed an indiscernible object flying at a distance. A sketch was also provided which depicted a ray-shaped anomaly.

8

SHAPESHIFTER ON THE TRI-STATE TOLLWAY

MY COLLEAGUE JAMIE BRIAN ran across the following account, which was part of a comment on a thread concerning the 'humanoids.' It seems the person who posted the account verified that she had posted it and that she swore the information was factual. I eventually got an email from the poster and had a brief conversation. Here's the account:

"Ok; this is crazy. Back on Feb. 8, 2017, just after 1 AM, I messaged a medium friend of mine. I'll copy and paste the message I sent:

"Hey, sorry to bother you, but you were the first person I thought to ask about this. What do you think of this and what do you think it means?

My husband John (who's a huge skeptic as we all know and doesn't believe in stuff like this) was just driving home in the dark and he saw what he thought was a person running on two legs across the highway and then it turned into a giant blackbird and flew up and away. He swears it was running on two legs, when it turned into the biggest bird he'd ever seen; flying with long legs?

What are your thoughts? Sounds creepy to me? Shapeshifter? Angel? Demon? He's totally creeped out. LOL."

We came to the conclusion that maybe it was a shapeshifter. This happened on I-294 (Tri-State Tollway) south near 111th shortly after midnight, between Worth and Chicago Ridge, IL.

Then today my friend messaged me asking if my husband thinks it's a Mothman. We Googled it and this popped up? Crazy! He said it sounds exactly like what he saw. My husband doesn't believe in stuff like this and when he got home he was white in the face with goose bumps. If anyone else had of told me what he saw, I wouldn't have believed it, but coming from my husband, I knew it was true.

What does everyone think it means? - JayJay."

Since this was a spontaneous comment on a thread not related to the Chicago sightings, I believe there is some legitimacy to the account. If it is connected with the current group of sightings, then it was the earliest in 2017.

ILLINOIS, Indiana and Wisconsin have a long history of strange flying anomaly encounters, especially when it pertains to huge black birds. There have also been occasional sightings of flying Pteranodon-like beings in and around Chicago.

Cryptozoologist and colleague Ken Gerhard recently shared the following account with me. It details a flying cryptid encounter near Chicago in 1969. The report was included in his book; 'Big Bird: Modern Sightings of Flying Monsters,' entitled; 'An Illinois Sighting (1969),' Park Forest, IL:

"I along with four of my friends saw a Pteranodon about three to four feet tall through the body around April of 1969; as memory serves it might have been 1970.

I do recall we were riding in my friend's 1969 Boss Mustang.

We were on a gravel road south of Park Forest, Illinois; a small suburb on the southside of Chicago. At that time there was nothing but country and farmland south of Park Forest. We were heading west on Stuenkle Road going to Monee, Ill.

We were in the valley a few houses west of where I used to live as a boy, I was like 17 or 18 years old. It was a foggy night, really thick blanket of fog close to the ground, as we started up the hill we emerged from the fog and it was a crystal clear night with a full or almost full moon and lots of stars.

We were driving along and my friend just slowed down and stopped the car. He leaned up over the steering wheel and stared at an angle out of the windshield.

I asked him what he was doing and he didn't answer me he just kept staring out the windshield, so I leaned forward and looked up and out of the windshield and silhouetted against the full moon, sitting on the top of a telephone pole was this Pteranodon.

The body was covered with fur like a bat, It had its wings folded up tight against its sides and you could see little claws at the top of each folded wing.

It had a tail similar in length to that of a cat in comparison to the body size, but it was smooth like a rat's tail except for a single tuft of hair at the very end.

As we sat there watching it, it was looking to the left and then to the right and then it would look off across the golf course to the north. The whole time it was switching its tail around like a cat does when they are aggravated, very nervous movements. *The neck and head were smooth leather like, no hair at all.*

I don't know exactly how long we sat there watching it, probably only a few minutes but it eventually looked down at us in the car and then threw its head back opened its mouth, showing very impressive teeth and let out a blood curdling screech and with three flaps of its wings did a half back over twist and sailed silently out over the field headed toward a large marsh south of our position and disappeared into the fog.

We were only thirty feet from the base of the phone pole and the pole was probably only twenty to twenty-five feet tall, so we were very close and got a real good look at the thing.

Over the years I have only shared this information with a few close friends and they treat me like I'm nuts. I am still friends with two of the guys I was with that night but we have never talked about what we saw that night.

Well, that's my story. I hope it helps." (Source: The Pterodactyl Society.)

THERE HAVE BEEN other Pteranodon-like sightings and encounters in the Chicago area. Vance A. Nesbitt, host of 'The Caravan of Lore' radio show and a member of the Chicago Phantom Task Force, had an interesting guest detail their encounter with an unknown winged creature.

Vance writes:

This story is from the later part of 2000. Tony grew up in the Chicago area and in his early 20's he attended the Chicago Job Corps school to advance his knowledge in the trades. The campus is off of Kedzie Ave. and the property is bordered by a tributary river.

"It was a sunny midday when Tony and a friend were having a cigarette and facing the river when they noticed a large shadow gliding over the ground. He felt it to be odd but didn't pay much attention since neither one looked up to see what it was. It was just a few moments later when both witnesses saw a large creature flying very close to the water surface of the river. Tony made first note of how odd this bird was because he thought it was a large tropical species. He was taken back as the bird drew closer. It was a murky green color; with scales on the body, but feathered wings. He stated that it had a very long tail, like a snake, with a small tufted feather on the tip.

This creature landed approximately thirty feet away from the two men when it began to use the claws on the leading edge of the wing to crawl up a small dirt rise. Tony mentioned that it truly reminded him of a prehistoric monster seen in books. This animal made its way to the top of a drain inlet where it had climbed inside. Tony's friend began to yell profanities and throw small rocks at the beast to try to draw it back out, but Tony cautioned him not to do that because this encounter scared him and he had no idea of what this thing could do to them if it came to attack. Tony estimated the wingspan to be five feet and the body to be between five to six feet.

This brief encounter left him stunned and very upset. He insisted that he never wants to see this creature ever again. The illustration is what I found that Tony says looks very close to what he saw. The drawing is what Tony did to illustrate how he saw the bird." Further north near LaCrosse, Wisconsin, in September 2006; a man and his son encountered a six to seven feet tall being with bat-like, leathery wings with a span of ten to twelve feet, long claws on its feet and hands and a snarling expression on the face. It flew towards their windshield, stared at them and then swooped upwards into the night sky.

Both witnesses became violently ill, and remained so for about a week. The man later told researcher Linda Godfrey that the winged being had distended ribs, long sort of human legs with claws, huge bat-like wings with 'arms' sort of attached. He remembered the teeth and the scream they heard was terrifying. It became known as the 'Man-Bat of Briggs Road.'

The man-bat account, in some respects, matches the current sightings in Chicago. The LaCrosse winged being displayed aggression and its presence caused the witnesses to become ill. So far that has been the case with the Phantom sightings. But as we go further along into the case log, the encounters do become more personal and frightening.

Another sighting soon emerged from Thursday, July 20, 2017, at approximately 5PM CT; it was reported to UFO Clearinghouse on August 1, 2017:

"We were driving down Lake Shore Drive toward North Avenue Beach. I was in the car with my best friend, my sister, and my boyfriend. As we were approaching the curve near North Avenue Beach, we saw something fly out from underneath the bridge that goes over the street that separates that big black building in front of Navy Pier (Lake Point Tower) and the beach. It flew straight up into the air and out toward the lake. This was not an owl and it was not a seagull, as seagulls are white in color. My boyfriend, who was in the front seat with me, was the first to see it and showed me. Everybody else saw it afterwards.

It was freaky as f*** to see this thing fly up like that. It was like completely black and look like a giant flying bat. It flew straight up and out of sight. I could not keep watching it as I was trying to drive and not get into a wreck. It was freaky to watch."

Manuel called the witness for a follow-up:

The witness states that they were on their way to a gathering with friends at North Avenue Beach. The entity shot out from what looked like under the bridge. It flew above the trees and headed out toward the lake. It was seen by the driver, who was trying to avoid hitting another car. The boyfriend said that it was solid black and was flying very fast.

This is practically the same location where this entity has been seen emerging previously. The Lake Shore Drive overpasses have been targeted by our team as possible portal locations. As I stated previously, there are several tunnels and underground facilities along this lake front area. We considered placing trail cameras in this area, but soon realized that this wasn't going to happen. First of all, the area is full of vagrants. Any cameras placed by us would have quickly been stolen. As well, the Chicago Police Department was not going to allow us to place anything on city property.

The city has a few security cameras in the area and in other locations of interest. I called and made an inquiry, asking for permission to examine the recordings. My request was noted and I was told that I would receive the proper request form in my email. So far, that hasn't happened, though I will continue to ask. I'm not holding my breath.

UFO CLEARINGHOUSE RECEIVED another sighting report on the same day as previous account:

"I was leaving work at about 8:45PM CT on Thursday night, July 27, 2017, in The Loop (central business section of downtown Chicago). As I walked the two blocks to the nearest train station to go home, I saw a large bat-like creature that was perched on top of one the streetlight poles across the street from the Harold Washington Library. This creature stood about seven feet tall and was sitting there motionless.

This creature had a pair of glowing red eyes that appeared to be fixated on something across the street. It stood there for about six-seconds. That's when I saw a flash from a group of kids on the sidewalk as someone was taking a picture of this thing. It then spread open a large pair of wings flapped them a couple of times and took off into the air. The girls from that group of kids screamed and they all took off running.

I saw as it shot up and over the library and was gone; in the matter of about two-seconds. I was very shaken up by what I saw and talked to my pastor about it at church on Saturday. It was he who pointed me in the direction of this site where I can make this report. Thank you."

At least one member of the clergy in Chicago was keeping tabs on the sightings. Since the witness stated that the group of kids had possibly taken a photograph of this being, I started posting on a slew of local chat boards and internet classified sites requesting photographic evidence. I had already been placing our contact information on social media and comment sections of blogs and websites that had been reporting the sightings.

By this time, as the result of me posting and announcing my telephone contact number practically everywhere possible, I was beginning to receive a large number of calls and texts from citizens in Chicago. They were worried that these sightings were a warning or omen of bad tidings for the city. From the third week of July until early September, I was receiving between ten to twenty calls per day. The 'Chicago Phantom' was becoming the word on the street; and people were damn scared!

9

HEADING TO THE SUBURBS

NOT TOO LONG after the Harold Washington Library sighting in downtown Chicago, I received a report that occurred in August 2016. The witness Tony G. was a security expert and worked throughout the city, especially at nightclubs and large lounges. Here is his account:

"Last summer, I believe in early August (2016), on my commute home I got off the bus and started walking about a block-and-a-half near W. Roosevelt Rd. and S. 59th Ave. in Cicero. It was a warm night and I could hear and see all the usual things happening (it wasn't unusual for me to see bats flying around and landing in or on a chimney). But this night something caught the corner of my eye. I figured it was just another bat and I really didn't pay it much attention. Then it happened again, but this time I had an eerie feeling come over me; like something was watching. Again I saw something swoop by, near an opening approximately fifteen feet above me and about ten feet to the right of me as I was facing south.

As I turned my head upward, I looked at the streetlight (that was across the street). I thought I saw something perched on top of it. I thought my mind was playing tricks on me. I started to squint to try to focus more on what I thought was on top of the streetlight and couldn't see it too well because the light was in my eyes. It was only when I raise my hand to partially block the light and I could see clearly there was something perched on the streetlight that was very large in size.

When I was finally able to see it better, it stood up. As I was stricken with fear and curiosity at the same time, I was able to see that its head came to a point with red-amber glowing eyes. It flapped its wings twice, and was airborne and took off towards the north.

This is the first time I've mentioned any of this to anybody, but when I read the article about other people seeing the same thing, I had that feeling of fear and curiosity come over me again and I felt was compelled to tell my story. I lost a lot of sleep over it trying to reconcile in my mind what I saw. It's real and when I came across the post, I got a flashback of what happened last year. - Tony G."

I was able to obtain Tony's telephone number and called for an interview. I posted the following information:

The witness works in security; and is apparently well-known in the club industry throughout Chicago. He was apprehensive about being ridiculed if he mentioned his experience. The witness was walking south on S. 59th Ave. when he had the encounter. He stated to me that the winged humanoid was dark in color, at least seven feet in height and that the wing span was approximately ten feet or so. It was perched on two human-like legs. He also mentioned that he noticed a short pointed crest on the head. There was no noise or sounds made by the being and when it ascended from the streetlight, it took two flaps of its wings and was swiftly aloft. He said that when this being looked at him, he instantly became frightened; and that this fear was imprinted on him. Tony was very forthcoming and didn't embellish his description of the being or the incident.

The witness mentioned a short pointed crest, and indicated that he was positive about what he observed. There had been a few other sightings on the edge of the city, including the incorporated town of Cicero. But we were about to receive a very close and personal account from a southwestern suburb, better known for a series of murders a decade before.

BOLINGBROOK, Illinois is an unassuming village with nice homes and well-kept parks. In 2007, the town was thrown into the national spotlight after a retired Bolingbrook police sergeant, Drew Peterson, was suspected in the disappearance of his fourth wife, and then was eventually convicted of drowning his third wife.

I'm quite sure that these events had nothing to do with the encounter I'm about to describe, but it was an interesting footnote that I recognized as soon as I heard the location.

I received a telephone call early Thursday, August 3, 2017, at 1:30AM ET from a distraught woman who wanted to tell me about an encounter that she had just a few hours before she contacted me. Her older son was also present, and was attempting to calm her as we talked. Here is a synopsis of our conversation:

The encounter took place in the playground area of Indian Boundary Park in Bolingbrook, Illinois; a southwest suburb of Chicago. The witness states that she has a normal routine of walking in the park at night. On Wednesday, August 2, 2017, at approximately 10:30PM CT (local time), the witness (who wishes to remain anonymous in the report since she resides in a tight-knit community) was in the playground area of the park when she came upon a seven to eight foot tall being standing in the middle of a pathway. The witness initially thought that this was 'two people embracing' but was surprised at the height. She also noticed a sucking and slobbering sound. She felt like she was 'drawn' to the being, as well as feeling a sense of foreboding and apprehension.

The witness grabbed her cell phone in order to capture a photo, but was shocked when the being slowly turned in her direction. Overcome with fear, she quickly realized that this was not two people embracing, but a single tall and wide dark humanoid. The witness got the feeling that it somehow knew that she was going to take a photo and then reacted. She mentioned that she felt like she was being 'lured' towards the humanoid. The being had exceptional broad shoulders and looked like it was wearing a thick black unknown material. The head was human-like but quite small in size. She was within fifteen feet of the being, but never noticed any eyes or facial features. There was enough moonlight available, so she was able to get an excellent look at this being.

She immediately cut across the grass and took another pathway in order to get away from the being. As she walked away, she soon began to experience intense weakness and fear. She had to sit and gather herself on a nearby bench, while keeping an eye out for the being. Eventually she was able gather herself and get to her feet; and quickly followed another path home.

When the witness arrived at her home, she relayed the experience to her son, who recommended that they drive back to the park and see if the being was still there. As they approached, they drove around the location. Then the son noticed a large dark shadow emerge from a nearby bush. It *stood up as he mentioned to his mother that it was 'peering' at him, though he didn't see any eyes or face. He just knew that it was watching him and that he was overcome by intense trepidation. They quickly left the area and headed home.*

When they arrived home, they were both very scared and upset; not knowing what to do. Should they report the incident to the local authorities or remain quiet? Eventually, they went online and found my contact information. When I talked to the witness, she was shocked after I told her about the number of sightings in the Chicago metro area. She had no knowledge of any of the previous incidents. It was quite obvious that she was still very frightened and mentioned to me that she was afraid that the being may know where she lives.

I asked the witness to keep in contact with me if she has another experience, hears of any other sightings or remembers further details.

At that point, this was the closet any of the witnesses had gotten this being. I believe that it may have been sleeping (while standing) when the witness walked up to it; as it made the bizarre sounds, possibly compared to those sounds a sleeping human would make if they were snoring or mumbling.

I asked the witness why she didn't immediately back away when she noticed how tall this being was. She stated that she had thought that this was two people embracing and that they had a partially opened umbrella extending above them. But as soon as it began to slowly turn in her direction, she knew that this was something else.

The park in which the playground was located is a large complex nearby a school and subdivision along Springwood Lane. I asked the witness if the covering may have been membrane-like wings wrapped around the body; in which she acknowledged in the affirmative.

THIS ENCOUNTER DESCRIPTION reminded me of other witness reports that I have received over the years, especially a report that was forwarded to me by the Munroe Falls Paranormal Society in September 2009:

"MFPS was contacted by a person who had an extremely odd sighting of an entity here in Stow, OH, an adjacent community of my hometown. Witness' wife contacted me with the story and after several days of negotiation, the witness agreed to meet with me, recreate the events and answer questions. Witness was extremely hesitant, but his wife persuaded him to recall the encounter.

On the night of 9/14/09, the witness, who wishes to remain anonymous, was driving to work. It was approximately 10:15PM, and he was northbound on Hudson Drive. As the witness drove under the RT 8 overpass bridge, just north of the Hudson Drive Applebee's Restaurant, he witnessed a nine to ten foot tall solid black entity standing on the southbound side of the road. No discernible head or facial features noticed. The duration of the sighting was approximately five to ten-seconds. The distance was approximately fifteen to twenty feet from his vehicle.

The witness had the feeling the entity was watching him and was "there" for him only. No other vehicles/persons were present during sighting. Immediately after turning his head back to the road, he looked in rearview mirror, but entity no longer visible. He did not see the entity depart or disappear.

Witness became extremely upset and scared. He felt that he had become pale, and his eyes began to water uncontrollably.

His first thought was to turn around and go home, calling off of work. He tried to call his wife at home, but his cell phone would not work, either from the programmed address book, or manual input calling. He continued getting a "call failed" notification, which had never happened before. The cell phone continued to be affected all the way to the I-271 entrance ramp, approximately eight to ten miles up the road.

The witness did make it to his job, but has since regretted not turning around and going home, due to his state of mind. The experience was traumatic in every sense of that word. It was a "bad" night for him at work. Weather was clear and the stars were visible. Other than the uncontrollable watering of the eyes, there were no other physiological or physical effects on his person. Though the cell phone was not working, there were no other effects noticed on inanimate objects, such as streetlights, car, or timepiece (watch). There was no known memory lapse, no dreaming related to the sighting as of this report. No overt paranormal experiences were reported during his normal daily life.

The witness stated that immediately after the sighting he became more and more agitated and scared the further he drove along. He had a distinct feeling that the entity was waiting for him and possibly following him, but he did not see it again that night. There have been no disturbances at witness' place of residence.

The following day on his way home, as he neared the RT 8 overpass, this time driving over the bridge he went under the day before. As he approached the bridge area, his eyes began to water uncontrollably once again, as he drove over the bridge and his eyes continued to water, until he passed beyond the bridge, when his eyes began to clear up.

Witness provided me a pencil drawing of what he observed. The drawing bears an uncanny resemblance to the original drawing submitted by an original Mothman witness of Point Pleasant WV in 1966. The witness is willing to keep me informed of any further sightings or activity. I believe I have gained his trust, as I mentioned he wasn't really interested in coming forth with this. My intuitive reaction is that witness is extremely believable and honest in his testimony. There were no outrageous embellishments to either his story, which I asked him to relate twice, nor to his drawing, which was really rather simple in nature.

So to this end, there are no answers at this point. But the eerie drawing he provided and its uncanny resemblance to the Mothman legacy are very much intriguing. I will continue to correspond and follow up with the witness periodically and will be anxiously waiting to see if any other sightings are reported in this vicinity that might validate this entity's appearance."

The sketch drawn by the witness in Stow, OH is very similar to what the witness in Bolingbrook encountered. There have been other similar sightings reported to me in the past, but this particular account has always stuck with me. The Stow witness also described his physical and emotional reaction to this being as well; another similarity to several of the Phantom encounters.

WITNESS DRAWING 9/23

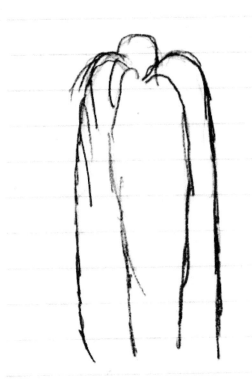

Stow, OH witness sketch.

On Saturday, August 4, 2017, UFO Clearinghouse received a report of a 'large black bat' over a Melrose Park shopping center parking lot. This particular location is very near

Manuel's residence, so he quickly drove to the parking lot in order to gauge what had happened. But this time around, there was a photograph taken. It wasn't an ideal image, but it did give us some indication of what the witness stated and that this winged being had considerable size to it. Here's the report:

> "I would like to report a sighting that I had today in downtown Melrose Park, Illinois at Winston Plaza (1254 Winston Plaza, off Rt.64
>
> W. North Ave.), on Saturday, August 4, 2017, just outside the Best Buy store.
>
> I was coming out of the Best Buy with my husband when we saw what looked like a large black bat that flew over the building. It must have been at least 20 feet or more up in the air and was solid black and flying very fast.
>
> I reached for my phone to try to get a picture of it, but by the time I fished out my phone from my purse, unlocked it and pulled up the camera, the bat had flown quite a distance away from us. I was able to snap one good picture of the object before it got too far away from us. I am not the greatest photographer and my cell phone is a couple of years old already, but you can see the object in the picture flying off to the east toward the city. I did not see a lot of detail. I do remember it was solid black, bigger than any bird I have seen and had a large pair of wings that must have been seven feet wide.
>
> I hope the picture helps in telling what it was or was not."

It was later determined that the incident occurred during the late afternoon, approximately 5:00PM CT.

All micro-bats and macro-bats (Flying Fox Bats) are nocturnal flying mammals. They roost during the daylight hours and feed at night. Theories that these may be macro-bats that escaped from a zoo or that it may possibly be someone's pet, just doesn't hold water.

Could it be an unknown species of flying mammal? I suppose that is a possibility. But the discovery of a previously unknown species of macro-bat in the Chicago area seems to be a bit of a stretch. Since a large flying mammal would most likely originate and thrive in a tropical environment, Chicago just doesn't seem to be an ideal situation.

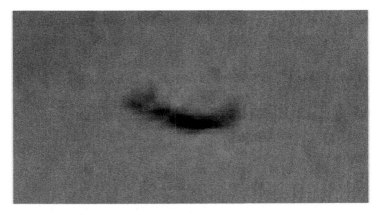

Photograph of winged being in Melrose Park, IL.

Photographic analysis of the image determined that it wasn't manipulated in any manner. As well, it became obvious that the subject in the photograph was a living entity and not an airplane or inanimate object.

We now had an indiscernible photograph and several sketches; not ideal, I'll admit, but the witnesses' reasons for not obtaining an image of the being did seem legitimate. All that we could do was hope that a future witness would get an opportunity to document this winged anomaly in an image.

ON SATURDAY AUGUST 5, 2017, a report surfaced on the MUFON CMS of a dramatic encounter with a giant bat in the Park Forest neighborhood:

River Forest, Illinois, Friday August 4, 2017, 5:30PM CT (local time): "I walked with my three girls to the corner 7-11 after my oldest got out of soccer practice. We usually do this after each one has practice as a little treat run before walking home. This day was overcast and quite a bit cooler than the previous days, which were very hot and muggy. After we got our Slushies and other snacks, we proceeded to walk home along the usual route which takes us past the practice fields at Dominican University.

We were all talking and laughing when I spotted what looked like a giant bat flying just above the treetops at the corner of Division Street and Williams Street where we cross the road to head toward home. I showed it to my girls as the bat turned toward where we were standing. This sudden move scared my five and seven year old who cowered down and screamed. The bat was flapping its wings and flew above us and then over the football field. It then banked and flew off in a southwestern direction and disappeared over some treetops. We stood there for about two-minutes stunned, before I collected my girls; who were scared and sobbing. We continued the rest of the way home.

The bat looked like it had human-like arms and legs, just a lot bigger and had a large pair of bat-like wings that it flapped as it flew. It was black with some grey, but there were no distinguishable features.

I know what I saw was real and had to be a living creature. There was no sound, but it was a solid object. I asked each of my girls to describe what they say saw and they all agreed that it looked like a huge black bat. They were very scared and I had to explain to them that we might have just seen a very big bat and there was nothing to be scared of."

Like I had stated previously, the encounters seemed to be getting more personal, and this winged being was not shy about showing itself.

Since this report was submitted to MUFON, we were not privy to contact information. But I did examine the area through

Google maps, and was able to determine that the account was very credible.

An important attribute to this particular sighting is that it occurred on the say day as the Melrose Park incident and only thirty or so minutes later. The distance between the locations in Melrose Park and River Forest is a mere three miles. The winged being could have easily covered the distance within the time period. It seems that we could most likely confirm that the two incidents were generated by the same flying humanoid.

Another oddity that may or may not be related to this sighting is that I sensed the words 'Dominican' and 'University' while conducting a remote session the day before for the Drenning case. The Drennings are a couple who had a horrific entity encounter in one of the TNT bunkers near Point Pleasant, WV several years ago. They continue to experience paranormal related activity. I went back to check; and the words were in my session notes. This is just another bizarre facet of the 'Chicago Phantom' flap.

MANY OF THE Mothman-like encounters that I have reported over the years involve aggressive behavior. For example; an experiencer forwarded an encounter report that demonstrates its intrusive nature:

> "Hello, a friend suggested I write to you about something that happened to me several weeks ago. I am divorced and have two boys; 15 and 12 years old. Both of my sons were with me at the time of the incident. We live in Huntington, West Virginia; moved here in 2009 from Milwaukee, WI because of my job.
>
> On March 2, we were traveling south on Rt. 2 (Ohio River Rd.) just outside of Huntington near Cox Landing Rd. It was

around 8:30 PM; we were on our way back home after visiting a co-worker. About a mile past the intersection I noticed something flying from behind a house on the right side of the road. It was hard to make it out at first but as it came towards the road, it looked like a huge butterfly. Even though it was dark, the light from the side of the house illuminated it enough that I could make out a shape.

I sped up to avoid coming in contact with this thing but as I did it circled around and flew just ahead of us on our right side. The wings were enormous and broad like that of a butterfly. It was strange because I never saw it flap the wings; almost like it was gliding. My boys were now aware of it and were terrified. I didn't want to stop the car so I decided to speed up some more. After about twenty-seconds it suddenly shot up into the air and disappeared.

One thing I want to mention is that we were under severe storm and flash flood warnings that evening. There were some high wind gusts and hail. There had been several tornadoes southwest of us in Kentucky. When we got home we talked about it. My oldest boy said it looked like a person dressed in a black shiny suit. He didn't see legs or feet but said the body shape looked like a tall thin man. My youngest boy said he didn't get a very good look but felt like something bad was going to happen. My description is very similar to my oldest son's, but the wings were massive and broad. I'd say the wings may have been over twice the size of the body. The entire thing was dark colored but there was a faint orange glow from the head area. I never noticed a face or other features.

Last week I was talking to a friend and told her about the incident. She found your name and contact information and forwarded it to me. She mentioned something about Mothman sightings in this area and I read some of the stories. I'm not sure if this is the same thing but it does fit the description.

There were a few drawings on Google. Some are close to what I saw but don't generally match the wing size.

If you have questions please use my email. I'm more curious of what I saw and anything else you can offer. I don't want to believe the Mothman stories but maybe you have an explanation. Thank you for your time. - NR."

I later called the witness and explained that there have been several closely related encounters in the Ohio River Valley. The aggressive behavior is indicative and akin to what the original Mothman witnesses described. Many people believe that the flying humanoid sightings around Point Pleasant, WV and the surrounding counties ended after the collapse of the Silver Bridge. That is simply not the case. These sightings and encounters continue to this day:

"Hello Sir, I wish to report 'something' I witnessed on March 17, 2017, near my home. I live in a rural area in Cabell County, WV. I am a widow and moved to this house last September 2016, from Ohio. I live with my daughter.

Not long after we moved in, we began to hear loud 'flapping' sounds coming from the river across the road from my property. The sounds would usually occur at night. We also saw bright orange lights through the trees near the river.

One afternoon I walked across the road and looked around, but I couldn't find anything out of the ordinary.

The sounds and the lights continued all winter. In fact, one evening while it was snowing, the flapping sounds were very loud. I watched from my living window as a bright orange light quickly moved upstream, then downstream above the river.

Then on Friday, March 17, I was on my front porch and heard a loud 'squawk' come from the direction of the river. I *looked that way and saw a huge bird-like 'something' above the trees. It was early evening, but it was silhouetted against the sky. It looked like it stopped in mid-flight, stretched its wings and hovered in mid-air. It had bright orange lights or eyes and seemed to stare and radiate at me. It was terrifying and menacing! I ran into the house and called for my daughter who was in the basement. We looked out the window, but it was gone.*

We haven't heard any sounds or seen any lights in the two weeks since my sighting. Can you tell me what I saw? - JL."

I emailed JL; then I later called her. She stated that the creature resembled a huge wasp and hovered like a flying insect. The thin body was tapered and the wings were solid. I asked her if it was shaped like a butterfly or moth; she acknowledged it had a similar outline, but only two large wings. She estimated that the wing span was ten to twelve feet and that the body was about four foot in length. There was no head, but the bright orange 'eyes' were positioned within the body. It was dark in color and the wings were more 'rounded' and 'solid' as compared to a butterfly or moth. She also noticed that there were several thin arm-like 'things' sticking out from the mid-body.

The witness sounded quite rational, but truly worried that this creature would return. She swears that it looked directly at her, leaving her with a feeling a dread and fear. She estimates that she was about forty yards or so from it.

I asked her to keep in contact with me and to report any unusual activity in and out of the house. She did acknowledge that the house is spiritually active and that she has witnessed a shadow being on three occasions. There have not been any disturbances affecting her sleep or daily routine. Her daughter has not experienced any of the activity.

The description is somewhat similar to the Mothman

encounters that have been reported to me in the past; though this particular being is smaller than those previous reports. Could it have been a misidentified bird, owl or custom-built drone? It does seem unlikely.

I ALSO RECEIVED an account from an area upstream from Point Pleasant along the Kanawha River:

"In September 2014, I was visiting friends in Fayette County, West Virginia. I once lived there when I was boy and this was the first time I had been back since I left for college in 2005.

My favorite pastime back then was to fish the Kanawha River, especially near the falls and up river in the deep water.

On my way home, I stopped off the point downriver from the falls and walked around. It was overcast and starting to turn to dusk. As I looked upriver towards the falls I saw something flying over the river near the opposite bank. It was flying south along the bank over houses and the railroad tracks. It then banked and turned towards my direction. The closer it got to me I started to realize how large it was. The body was black and was shaped like a cylinder tapered to a pair of short legs. The feet were tucked up so I was unable to describe those. It didn't have much of a tail that I could see. The wings were wide and broad, but I never saw it flap. It was floating and barely moving the wings. It was the strangest thing I've ever seen. As I thought about it later; the wing span was at least twenty feet. The texture was similar to leather though the low light made it difficult to see. I couldn't see a defined head or other features as it flew above me and beyond the trees. I wasn't scared but amazed. I can't give you an idea of what this was. I never heard any sound. I didn't see it again.

A week later I called my aunt who lives upstream from the falls and mentioned it to her. She said that she had never heard anything about large birds. I'm not sure this was an actual bird because it didn't fly like one. It seemed to propel by other means. - Cameron."

I was eventually able to talk to the witness by telephone. He couldn't recall any further information, but I'm convinced that the size of the unknown flying being was quite large. If the wings had a twenty foot span, I'd speculate the body was at least six feet long according to the description.

NOT UNLIKE THE Mothman of Point Pleasant, later encounters have included a few strange circumstances. I received an email from a woman in Ohio who had concerns that pertained to an encounter her and a girlfriend had six months prior to the report:

"Sir, my name is Megan. I am forwarding a summary of an experience that I and a friend had in August 2010. My friend and associate Kyra and I traveled from Columbus, Ohio to Ravenswood, West Virginia on business. While we were there, I wanted to make a side trip to Gallipolis, Ohio in order to visit relatives I had not seen for quite a while.

After our meeting and presentation, we drove onto Ohio Rt. 7 and traveled south along the Ohio River towards Gallipolis. We had a nice, though brief, visit with my relatives. Around 6PM, we left their home and drove a few miles north on Rt. 7 to check-in to a hotel near the local airport.

Around 7:30PM, we decided to get dinner and found a quiet restaurant so we could eat and work. After we finished,

Kyra needed to go to the store and pick up a few items that she forgot to pack. We headed to a Wal-Mart that was nearby the restaurant.

After we finished shopping, we were walking to the car when I noticed a woman running through the parking lot. When she reached her car, she looked back in the direction of the store then hurriedly got into the car. I quickly looked in the same direction and saw what looked like a large bird flying above the roof of the store. It was difficult to see but when it swooped downward the parking lot lights would shine off of it. It looked like it was either oily or had shiny leather-like skin. Whatever it was, it had a wide wing span. I would guess it reached eight to ten foot across. It circled above the store for about a minute then just disappeared.

We were both somewhat shocked at what we witnessed but figured that it was just a huge bird. Since it was dark, I figured we had misjudged what it really was.

We drove back to the hotel and decided to call it a night so we could get an early start on the drive home in the morning. I got ready for bed but thought I'd watch some television first. By this time it was around 10PM or so.

I must have dozed off fairly quickly because the next thing I remember is frantic knocking on my door. I stumbled out of bed and checked who it was. It was Kyra and she was obviously upset. She rushed into my room and said, "It's here!" "What are you talking about?" I was a little bit perturbed that she woke me up. She said that she was lying on the bed reading when she heard something in the hallway. She got out of bed, walked to the door and listened to what she thought was 'scratching' sounds.

After a few minutes the sounds stopped, so she went back to bed. Not long after she laid down she heard more scratching sounds but, from outside her window. Again she got up and peeked through the curtains. This time, something looked back at her.

Our rooms were on the second floor in the back section of the hotel and both looked out onto a small parking lot and a large field beyond that. She could see, what she described as, a 'bald ugly man with wings' who was looking directly at her with 'large bulging eyes that lit up bright red.' It was there for only a few seconds. It then spread its wings while running at the same time towards the end of the parking lot, as it lifted off the ground like a bird.

"You're kidding, right?" I muttered to her. "Meg, I swear to God; that thing is out there and it knows we saw it!" I knew the only way I was going to get some sleep was to allow Kyra to stay in my room. The next morning we woke early, checked out and drove back to Columbus.

Kyra didn't mention the incident from the previous night during the ride. In fact, she has still never said anything else about it. We continue to be good friends and have a very good working relationship. But I was curious. I had never heard about the Mothman or any of the tales associated with it. I grew up in Texas and had only lived in Ohio for a few years. I moved into my Mom's house after she had passed away. Her relatives lived throughout Ohio but I had never been told any of the stories. This is the reason I am writing to you. We were near Point Pleasant, WV, when we had this encounter. Do you think that it is possible that this was a Mothman? I read some of your posts recently and I'm starting to believe that Kyra actually saw something supernatural.

In light of the prophecies of danger that this thing is supposed to warn people about, Kyra has had some bad luck and tragedy since that day. Her husband suddenly left her, she had a fire in her house and she severely injured her leg in a fall. Could this be connected?

I personally don't believe in predictions, either good or bad. But I will admit that these have been strange times since we witnessed 'whatever.'

I'm afraid I responded to Megan's concerns with a lot more uncertainty. We really don't have many answers for the Mothman. This group of sightings in the Chicago has raised more questions than answers at this point.

AROUND THE SAME period of time that the Melrose Park and River Forest encounters occurred, I received an email from a witness (BW) near Elgin, Illinois:

"I may have seen the being gliding west, away from Chicago. I work in Elgin about one mile north from I-90 and about forty-five minutes northwest of Chicago. I was outside of my work and looking skyward at the time. The being was very high up but I could tell it was very big, but it was an odd shape. It was at the height of mid-flying airplane. This was right around 11:45 AM on August 1, 2017. It looked just like the thing in that picture that you have on the first sighting (2011). It looked darker though, but that could have just been the distance that it was. And because it was high and it was going away from me also. I was hoping it would turn around but it just kept going on a straight glide westward. I was getting my phone out too late it would have looked like a dot if I would have tried to get a picture, that's why I was hoping it would turn around. I didn't notice it flapping its wings, so that's why I keep saying that it was gliding. It kept in a very straight direct motion. I plan on taking breaks for the next few weeks around this time in case it passes again.

Since this day it has been very cloudy so I haven't been able to get a good look at the sky, but I believe I might have seen it in the distance the next day playing in the clouds. If it is a creature of habit I hope it'll keep passing around my area around the same time. Like I said I saw something that looked like a person in one of those squirrel suit but if you know the suburbs, there is probably no way it could have been.

I have been watching the skies even closer since then and at this point I want to say whatever I saw would have been the size of a small plane possibly. But I didn't have anything to reference the size since it was so far up."

I was able to contact BW by telephone a few days later. He told me that the sky was cloudless and very clear. The color of the being, he believes, was very dark brown or black. It was flying very steady and effortlessly, but he was very doubtful that it was a person in a flying suit. He compared the shape to that of the photo from 8/22/2011 at 63rd and Pulaski Rd in Chicago, IL; which the Tasmanian witness stated that it looked like an 'over-size Tasmanian Sugar Glider.' BW refused to change his testimony has to what he originally witnessed. He also stated that he saw several birds flying at the same time and the size comparison was 'shocking' to him. The size of this being could have been much larger than the previous sightings.

In early September, Manuel was being interviewed on an internet radio show, along with the Illinois MUFON State Director. Like I have stated previously, MUFON has demonstrated vague interest in this phenomenon; but true to form, they were going to do all they could to discount the Phantom's existence. MUFON's contention was that this was a misidentified bird, namely a Great Blue Heron. The average fully grown adult Great Blue Heron stands three to four and a half feet, a wingspan of five to six and a half feet and weighs anywhere from four to eight pounds. Since none of the witnesses stated that they observed a long beak or neck, I believe it's safe to assume that this winged being is not a Great Blue Heron. Then the conversation was directed to the 2011 photograph.

The MUFON State Director empathically stated that the object in the photograph was a kite. He gave out a manufacturer name (Gayla) and a model number. I know that Chicago is known as the 'Windy City,' but on this particular warm August 22, 2011, the air was still. The wind speed averaged four miles per hour for the entire day. These are not ideal kite flying conditions.

My family has been in the hobby and collectible business since 1954, and we continue to maintain a brick and mortar store. Gayla kite kits have been a staple part of the inventory since the late 1960s. In fact, the triangular shaped, bird-like models were very popular. To make a long story short, my father never throws anything away; and our storage room currently houses a fair amount of Gayla kites and catalogs. I also searched online for any type of kite that matched the 2011 photograph's description, including professional stunt kites. None were to be found. This was another false narrative by the MUFON State Director. The facts don't lie.

10

CONFRONTATION

ON MOST OCCASIONS when the subject of the 'Chicago Phantom' sightings would be brought up during an interview or conversation, the references to the Mothman of Point Pleasant would soon become part of the discussion. The Mothman had a habit of swooping down onto vehicles, landing on car hoods and aggressively chasing frantic witnesses out of the West Virginia Ordnance Works and along Potters Creek Rd. The winged beings in Chicago, to this point, just weren't that intrusive.

An incident on the evening of Wednesday, August 9, 2017, changed the narrative. This time, the Phantom was going to make sure that it was seen, recognized and remembered.

I received a brief email on Thursday, August 10, 2017, at 3:45PM ET from a witness in Chicago. I was asked to call them for further information, so I responded with a telephone call within a few minutes:

> *The witness, 'AG' (actually the initials of witness' maiden name) and her husband (who both live in the Washington, DC suburbs), were in Chicago visiting her parents, who live at 1400 Lake Shore Dr. She was born and raised abroad, and her*

parents were now living in Chicago. 'AG' had an Eastern European accent, but she was comprehensible and fluent in the English language.

She stated that last night (Wednesday 8/9/2017) at approximately 9:20PM CT, the witness and her husband were returning to her parent's residence after taking a brief walk along N. Lake Shore Dr. (walking south). As they approached E. Schiller St. they noticed something large and dark flying towards them from their left (from the direction of Lake Michigan). Both witnesses were startled, as the flying anomaly crossed ahead of them at an altitude of twenty or so feet.

They watched the anomaly sweep upwards, over the trees in front of 1400 N. Lake Shore Dr., then stop in mid-air after it reached a height just a few stories from the top of the building. It hovered with a large pair of wings for approximately five-seconds, as it seemed to focus on the windows in front of it. It then bent backwards and fell into a dive down towards the trees. The witnesses hurriedly walked in the direction of the intersection and then turned right onto E. Schiller St., quickly heading towards the entrance to the condominium building.

THE YELLOW CIRCLE INDICATES THE LOCATION OF THE ENCOUNTER

Then suddenly, the large winged being slowly descended in front of them; no more than twenty-five feet away. It hovered about five feet above the sidewalk, with its wings spread open, as it peered at the couple with large bright red eyes that slowly altered back and forth in intensity.

Several people on the other side of the street, including a delivery van driver, reacted with screaming and frightened gasps. The winged being hovered for ten-seconds, then quickly pulled the wings into its body and shot up quickly into the night sky. There was no sound, other than a rush of air as the being flew upwards.

The witness 'AG' described the winged being as 'human-like' with a small head that narrowed at the top. It had legs like a human with long feet that tapered. Neither witness noticed any arms. The body was five to six feet in height and it had wide wings that resembled the top wings of a butterfly, attached along the length of its body. The illumination from the building entrance could be seen through the wings, so it looked to be made of a skin or membrane. The wing span was easily ten plus feet. The legs pulsated as it hovered in the air.

The overall color was very dark; like a deep bluish-green. The skin on the body may have been moist, since it was shiny. The eyes were large compared to the head size; slightly slanted, and alternated back and forth in brightness. It made no noise, other than a slight humming from the pulsating legs. Both witnesses stated that they felt a vibration that emanated from the being.

The witness did see at least one camera flash come from across the street. Neither witness was able to retrieve their phone. The fear and shock was too profound during the encounter. 'AG stated that she literally 'fell to her knees' after the incident, and that her husband had to assist her while walking the rest of the way to the building. Neither witness has slept more than an hour or two since their encounter eighteen hours previous.

The witness' statement by telephone was quite dramatic and detailed. I'll admit she freaked me out a bit. This encounter / sighting, to date, offered the best description of this flying humanoid. The witness' husband talked briefly, but he acted like he'd rather not say too much. The witnesses were scheduled to fly home the day I talked to them, but they delayed their departure for a few days. 'AG' told me "I'm just not ready to get on an airplane right now."

During the conversation, I soon discovered a possible reason why the witness' husband was reluctant to discuss the encounter. He is a fairly well-known professional athlete, though I never let on that I was aware of his identity.

Regardless of who the witnesses are, they were clearly upset by the encounter from the previous night. It was obvious 'AG' was continuing to suffer physical and emotional trauma, just by the way she would occasionally stammer when answering my questions.

The being's pulsating legs, that also made a humming sound, was a new detail in this sightings saga. I don't believe that I have ever seen or heard a similar element in any of the flying humanoid encounters I've been given in the past. A vibration emanating from the winged being and felt by the witness has been known to occur.

———

FIVE DAYS previous to this encounter, I had received a brief report from the evening of Saturday, August 5. The witness lives one block away from 1400 N. Lake Shore Dr. I was hoping to get more information through an interview, but the witness never got back to me:

> "I tuned to WGN Radio this morning around 4:15 CST and to my amazement heard you talk about the big moth being in Chicago.
>
> I saw something weird yesterday evening out my window. I live at 1350 N. Lake Shore Drive and was looking out my window over to the condos at Ritchie Court. At about floor 17, I saw reflected in that window, some dark blue wings pass by. First it went one window, then the next. And then a few seconds later, it went by another window. It was flying! I thought it was someone shaking a towel, but everything inside me said it was a flying moth! - C."

I was going to ignore the report because the witness never got back to me, and because I wanted more details. But in light of the 1400 N. Lake Shore Dr. encounter, I went ahead and posted both accounts together.

———

ON SATURDAY, August 12, 2017, UFO Clearinghouse obtained an account from a witness on the lake front, who also

added a bit of insight on how the city government was reacting
to the sightings:

> "I wish to report an incident that I had on Thursday (August
> 10, 2017) at about 7:30PM CT (local time) in Chicago. I was
> out walking my dog and was watching storm clouds as they
> were coming in. It was then that I saw what I can only
> describe as a big owl that was in the sky above the lake just
> offshore of Ohio Street Beach. It was flying in a circular
> pattern and looked like it was riding thermals as it was not
> using its wings much to keep it aloft but only gliding. I
> watched it for about a minute before it dipped down toward
> the shore and was out of sight.
>
> I waited around for about five minutes; even walking the
> half block over toward Lake Shore Drive to see if I could
> maybe see something from that vantage point. I saw nothing
> else and then headed home as there was a storm approaching
> and I did not want to be caught outside in the rain. I had heard
> several stories regarding these sightings but never thought I
> would have one myself.
>
> I did not see a lot of detail other than it was black with
> wings. It was large as it stood out against the sky and you
> could tell that it was using its wings in flight. I tried to rule out
> a larger than normal seagull or maybe somebody hang-gliding,
> but none seemed to fit what I had seen. I'm reporting this to
> you to add to your growing list of sightings within the city. I
> ask that I not be contacted in regards to this or that my name
> not be used. The reason being is that I work for the City of
> Chicago, within city government as administrative staff, and
> do not want this to get out and potentially jeopardize my job. I
> am very sincere in my sighting and wish to share it with you,
> but cannot risk losing what has taken many years to
> accomplish.

I can tell you that these sightings have not gone unnoticed and have garnered much attention, but there are powers to be that do not want the increasing number of sightings to jeopardize the summer by potentially scaring away tourists. But please know that these sightings have not gone unnoticed within City Hall."

This witness expressed the same sentiments concerning the local government that other city workers had been telling me for several months. I'm not sure that the witness was over-reacting, stating that they could lose their job, but I'll take them at their word. The Task Force had discussed the supposed reaction by the city officials, and we were a bit bewildered by their attitude. I was aware that a few of the aldermen on the City Council were checking into the reports, but it seemed to be a cursory effort. I hadn't heard about any commotion coming from the Cook County Board of Commissioners, but I'm keeping my ear to the ground.

SINCE THE TIME I started receiving and posting the flying humanoid reports from in and around the Chicago area, there have been several reports that weren't specific (or believable) enough to be considered as part of the mix. But there have been other sighting accounts that deserved to be mentioned as part of the record. Here are a few of those reports:

"I was getting out my car outside of the Target store in DeKalb, IL last week (Saturday afternoon, August 4; between 6:30- 6:40PM) when I noticed a couple were using their phones to video record something in the sky. I looked in that direction and there was something (someone) floating/flying

above and behind the storefronts. It was far enough away to not make out too many details but close enough that it definitely looked like a flying person with both arms and legs outstretched (looked like a flying X). My recollection is that it was mostly dark but there was some color reflecting from it in the afternoon sun; orange or red-orange.

It kind of "floated" horizontally away to the right, moving away from us (but never descending; therefore I figured it was being controlled somehow, not someone in a glider). At times it turned horizontal to the horizon, so you couldn't detect the shape. I did ask them; "What was that?" and they replied that they had no idea, but said it looked like a human with both arms and legs extended. I agreed.

I didn't catch a cell phone photo until it was too far away to make out the shape. I wish I knew who the people were that filmed it from right beyond the buildings. - AN."

I talked to 'AN' by telephone for quite a long time. A photo was forwarded, but was nothing more than a tiny spot that showed no detail whatsoever. 'AN' stated that the flying anomaly was visible to her for over ten minutes (other people had been watching it before her). She also stated that it was definitely human-like and the body was about six foot in height. The wing span was wide and beyond the length of the body. The aerial maneuvers were 'unbelievable;' floating, hovering, vertical descending and ascending. As well, there was an intermittent flash of reddish-orange color.

It's difficult to determine what she and the other witnesses may have seen. I was hoping that another witness from the location would come forward.

I HAD ALSO RECEIVED a brief telephone call from a witness who had a sighting in 2014. I asked him to forward the information by email:

> *"I spoke with you around 6:50PM today (August 13) about my winged creature experience out here in Chicago. I mentioned I was a little late about it, as I never thought to go out of my way to report it on any site. But I remember back in October/November of 2014, near 18th St in the direction of downtown Chicago, where the moon was at night time, I saw a black silhouette of a humanoid winged creature that I jokingly called a "Shinigami" from the Death Note series. I saw it span across the moon for a quick second and then disappear. I called my buddy and told my wife as well about the incident. Figured this may be of some use. Thanks again, -DM."*

In Japanese mythology, Shinigami are gods or supernatural spirits that invite humans toward death, and can be seen to be present or interpreted to be present in certain aspects of Japanese religion and culture. Basically, they can be compared to a 'Grim Reaper.' In the 'Death Note' series these beings look for humans and then take their lives. The description is that of a ghoul-like entity with human features that possess eyes that are used to mesmerize their victims.

11

GARGOYLE ON THE ROOF

MANY OF THE flying humanoid accounts that I have received over the years referred to the being as a 'gargoyle.' We usually perceive a gargoyle as a grotesque carved human or animal face or figure projecting from the gutter of a building. But many witnesses swear that they are seeing living winged beings with the physical characteristics of the mythical creature.

On Monday, August 14, 2017, I received an eyewitness statement by email from a gentleman in Tinley Park, Illinois:

"Hello Mr. Strickler,

My name is OS and I believe I have seen the Mothman. My encounter took place back in March. It was in Tinley Park at the corner of 174th Place and 66th Ave.

I was walking my dog at around midnight and he suddenly stopped at the corner. As I looked down at him I saw him staring off. As I looked up I saw and heard something "swoooshhhh" overhead. I didn't know what it was. I have heard of big birds coming down and taking small dogs (we have a Pomeranian) so naturally I looked around more for what it may have been and began walking toward a tree in front of a house.

As I got to the tree I noticed my dog looking across the street. So I tried to see where he was looking. My eyes went up to the rooftop across the street and there is when I noticed something big on the top of the roofline. It was as if it was crouching. I didn't know what the heck it was, so I slowly moved toward it while fumbling to get my phone. As I turned the LED light on my phone, and aimed it at the roof (not a very bright light) I kept walking towards it.

As I got about halfway in the street with my dog behind me, it seemed to have shot up and then it took a sharp downward turn down behind that house. It was something big. As I have told people, as that thing was crouched on the rooftop, it was almost next to the chimney and it made the chimney look small. It actually reminded me of a gargoyle.

I've attached a rough "map" of where we were and from what direction it swooped down and what rooftop it landed on. I'm not sure if you'll believe me or not, but I'd like only my initials used if you plan on using this story. My wife is the one who told me about these encounters. Her and my mother-in-law where the first ones I told as soon as I returned from walking our dog. Thanks again. - OS."

I wanted to get a bit more detail on the sighting, so I sent OS a few questions. He quickly responded by email:

"Hello Lon,

It was March 16, 2017, right after 12:00AM. Our dog liked taking late night walks. From what I saw when it flew above us it was not black in color, it was more of a dark brown. Because at the corner where we were standing are telephone poles and a streetlight at the end of the street where we were. This helped in showing the color a bit.

It was hard to get a specific description of it. I just know that it was big. The way it sat on the roofline and the lights behind it from the train station and bars in the downtown area, that back lighting helped in me seeing the crouched positioning it was in. The way it was crouching, it had bold shoulders. Odd, kind of the way a wide gargoyle would be perched. I can't say the eyes were red though. It was just a slight reflection cat/dog eye reflection if you know what I mean. It was dark in color except for the reflections. That is the reason I was trying to get my phone out in order to try and shine more light at it. It was odd.

You'd figure that our dog would have been going nuts at it, but it wasn't. It seemed just as intrigued as I was. When it did leave the roof it kind of shot up a couple feet and then shot straight down behind the house. And it was gone.

I carried a stream light after that. But of course I didn't get to see it again. It was just strange to come back from Saudi Arabia where I was working, to be back in time to see my son born; then to see this being a week later. - OS."

The witness didn't seem to show much personal fear of this being, but he was worried that it may attempt to snatch his dog. This sighting was more further south than the previous incidents.

I pinpointed the neighborhood and the exact house on which this winged being perched. It's somewhat difficult to determine the size. But judging by an image of the roof and the chimney that it crouched next too, it was probably similar in size with previous sighting descriptions. I'd estimate it was in the six to eight foot height range.

HERE IS A SUPPOSED 'GARGOYLE' sighting from 2013 near Des Plaines, Illinois. This report was sent directly to me by the witness:

"On a summer evening in 2013, my son and I were leaving my friend's house just outside of Des Plaines, Illinois. Her driveway is about a 1/4 mile long. There are no lights along the driveway. About halfway to the road, my son yelled out; "What's that?" I was startled and slammed on my brakes. "What are you yelling for?" He said; "there; in the tree!" I answered; "What are you looking at?"

I glanced up into the tree, and noticed talons wrapped around the large lower branch. The tree was thick with foliage, so it was hard to make out what it was. I figured it was just an owl or eagle, but as we watched the tree began to move, like there was something very heavy in the tree. The headlights were pointed directly at the tree, so there was some light.

Then suddenly, a human-like figure dropped from the tree and landed upright on the ground in front of us. It was dark grey in color. As I looked at the clawed feet and muscular legs, I noticed the bottom tip of folded wings behind it. My eyes followed up the human-like body, which looked like dark grey skin. The head and face literally reminded me of a gargoyle; snarling features and evil-looking. The eyes were large and reflected an orange color. I believe it also had short horns on the side of the head. "OMG! What is that?" At the same time my son begged me; "Let's go! Let's go!" The beast opened its huge wings and literally took off up over the car!

I called my friend on my cell phone as we were driving home. I told her what we witnessed; she was totally dumbfounded. She told me that she had never seen anything *like that. While driving, I ask my son what he thought he saw. He called it a 'Batman.' I simply responded "OK," but I thought gargoyle or some other mythical creature. I was deeply affected by this beast and have carried this odd feeling that it would remember us.*

Now I've been reading about the sightings in Chicago, and wonder if there is a connection. I fear that a terrible event may occur in the city. My son is in college in Chicago, and I work downtown. I am scared for us. I swear what I have described is true. I wish to remain anonymous; and I don't seek any recognition."

The witness' email address was from a Chicago law firm; and since her name is part of the firm name, I can assume she is a partner. The description is similar to some of the recent sightings. Is there a connection? Well, there are old reports from in and around the Chicago metro area coming to our attention, so there may actually be some affiliation.

I'M FASCINATED by the gargoyle comparison made by witnesses of flying humanoids. For several years, a particular winged being has been seen in Butler County, Pennsylvania. The original report was submitted and investigated by Pennsylvania UFO and anomalies researcher Stan Gordon:

"On March 21, 2011, I was contacted by a witness who reported having an encounter with a very strange creature during the early morning hours of March 18, 2011. The incident occurred on a rural road in Butler County between Chicora and East Brady. The witness, a businessman passing through the area, stated that; "this was the freakiest thing I ever

saw, and it made the hair stand up on the back of my neck." The man told me that he was driving down the road when from about a ¼ mile away, he observed something on the right side in a grassy area. His first thought was that it was a deer. The driver stepped on the gas to move closer to get a better view. From about fifty yards away, he observed something that appeared to be hunched down, and then stood up. The driver then observed a very tall muscular creature.

At this point, the driver had his high beams on and watched as the creature walked in front of a yellow reflective road sign, then crossed the two lane road in three long steps and continued into a wooded area. What he saw was a humanoid figure that stood at least eight feet tall that appeared to have smooth leather-like skin that was of either a darker tan or light brown color.

The creature never looked at the witness, and was only observed from its side. The head appeared to be flat in the front section, and then rounded out. "At the top back of skull, it was like one of those aerodynamic helmets. The top was not quite a point, but looked like a ridge on top of the head." The face was flat, and the eyes were not clearly defined, but the man thought that they might have been pointed in the corner. The ear that was observed on the left side was long and flat, and came up and back and was pointed backwards like a flap.

The arms were muscular and a little longer than that of a human. The hands looked more like a claw, but the number of fingers was unclear. One physical trait that stood out were the extremely muscular legs. The witness stated that it was hard to explain, but the legs did not move like that of a human, and "looked like they bent backwards." The witness also saw what appeared to be wings on its back which were tucked into its body, with the wing tips extending toward the side of its head.

No unusual sounds or smells where noticed during the observation which was estimated to have been about seven to eight-seconds. As the motorist approached the location where the creature entered the woods, it could no longer be seen. The next day the witness decided to drive back to the location of the encounter to look for any evidence. The ground conditions were not suitable for tracks, and nothing was found. The witness did, however, measure the road sign that the creature had walked in front of. The sign was just over eight feet high, and the head of the creature was estimated to have reached about four inches above the sign. Stan notes later sightings reported to other investigators:

Since that initial report that I received concerning this strange encounter, it has been learned that other local residents from that same area also reported seeing a similar unknown creature. Dan Hageman, Director of BORU (Butler Organization of Research on the Unexplained), also received several reports from that same time period and general location. The following are some of the BORU summary reports on these incidents:

March 26, 2011, Kepple's Corner - Two witnesses were driving to Butler when they witnessed a dark tan, eight feet tall winged entity. The face appeared smashed in. It had a muscular body and a head that went to a point. The arms were long and it appeared to have claws for fingers. When it crossed the road it seemed to lope with each stride. The witnesses stopped the car in shock and sat there until another car came and they had to move. The witness is willing to take a lie detector test to prove what he saw.

March, 2011; East Brady - A witness was riding his motorcycle two miles past a custard stand and saw a large animal. It was bent over as if looking for something. As the witness got to within seventy-five feet of the creature it stood up. It was at least eight to nine feet tall, and the arms hung down below its knees. The skin looked like leather and it was very dark. Its eyes were swept up in the corners and it had a pointed head. It was very muscular and looked like it had wings on the side of its head. It also appeared angry. The creature then bolted into the woods. The witness stated that if anything it was straight from hell and it needed to go back.

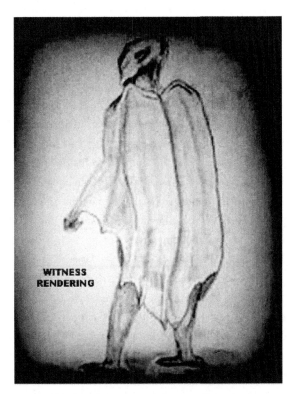

Witness sketch provided by Stan Gordon.

March, 2011; Rimersburg - Two witnesses had just left the ice cream stand headed for Rimersburg and noticed something crossing the road. They came to within about thirty-five feet of the creature. They stated that it was at least nine feet tall and had dark brown skin, long arms and broad shoulders. It had a pointed head, flat forehead, and pointed ears and what appeared to be wings on its back. The body was extremely muscular and there were four finger-like claws on each hand. The eyes were squinted but swept upwards at the corners. As the creature turned, the whole body would turn. The movement of the arms was not normal. The mouth looked like a slit. The wings looked like see-through mesh and resembled wings on a bat. The claws were black as coal. The witness stated that this thing was straight from hell. There is information coming in that a similar creature has been reportedly seen again in the same general areas of Butler County since about mid-July of 2012. Campers and others are rumored to have seen a strange large winged creature.

The original witness contacted me a few years later, in which he described his subsequent sightings:

"About two weeks later (two weeks after March 18, 2011, the original sighting) I was driving on the same road in the opposite direction. It was just after daylight. Not even a mile from initial spot of first sighting, I witnessed on my left in a field; the same creature hunched down about ten feet beside a round bale of hay. Even hunched down this thing was about three feet taller than the bale. It was looking straight at me. I did not notice any glowing or strangeness to its eyes. In the light of the morning and being to the west side of the bale it had a gray cast to it. Its hands/claws were black and down on the ground like you would see a gargoyle statue. There was not any snow on the ground, just the hay field and round bales.

I slowed down and watched it. The wings were partially seen on its back above the shoulders, just like a gargoyle statue.

About a month after that I witnessed it next to a wooded area in a hollow about five hundred yards from previous sighting. It was going into the woods around dusk. I saw it from the side and then its back as it entered the woods.

I know others have seen it as well. I intentionally left out details of my first sighting. I did not report my second or third sightings in order to wait and see if anyone else would report it. And if they did, what they had seen. I was hoping I was not the only one to see it. Turns out many people have seen it and a few reported it.

When I had my sighting I did not know where or who to report something like this to. After a search on the internet I found Stan Gordon's web site; so I asked him not to give out my name. I have heard from locals in the area that it's been seen for years.

There are many farms in this location and a family had a history of something going on, but never told too many people about it. I even did some research into the sightings. There are newspaper reports going way back of this. It's the same area the historic "Chicora Meteor" explosion took place. Although not related I did find out that in the 70's there had been a bunch of sightings of this and a hairy creature that is still seen north of there.

It was great to talk on the phone and know I am not the only one seeing these things. I am still looking into it. I had not been a paranormal or weird creature person. But after this, I have been trying to figure out what it is. - RK."

In February 2017, I received the following information:

"It was in 2013. My father worked at a company located off the road behind AK Steel in Lyndora, PA near Butler, PA. I was driving to pick him up from work one night and caught a glimpse of something in the sky. It was huge had wings of a prehistoric animal (Pterosaur) that looked to be around 8-10ft wing span! I never told my father what I saw right before I picked him up. It scared the crap out of me then and still does when I think of what I'd seen. -DM."

After I received the email from 'DM,' I sent a note to Stan Gordon, who verified that other similar sightings have occurred in the same general area. This winged being is referred to as the 'Butler Gargoyle.'

'LOLLAPALOOZA' is a huge annual summer music event that is staged in the lake front parks in Chicago's central business district. The Chicago Phantom decided to partake in the 2017 version of the festivities. The following report was forwarded to UFO Clearinghouse:

"My friend and I were attending Lollapalooza last Sunday, August 6, 2017, at Grant Park in Chicago. As the concert ended and we were walking back to the hotel, we saw what looked like a giant bat flying just above the tree tops in the park. As we walked into a clearing we saw that this thing had landed and was looking directly at us with a pair of glowing red eyes. These eyes were brightly lit and a brilliant red. We both screamed which attracted the attention of a few people who ran up to us and saw this thing. This thing then spread its wings open and shot straight up into the air.

It flew above the tree tops and then disappeared into the

darkness of the night. The strange thing, asides from this creature, was that the park was absolutely silent after it left. No birds were heard, not even the sound of the city around us; just a bunch of scared people trying to make heads or tails of what the hell we saw.

The creature was approximately seven feet tall and was completely black. It had a pair of red eyes that glowed and when its wings spread open it must have been at least ten feet across. These wings did not look like they had feathers but instead looked like what a giant bat's wings would look like. It made no sound other than the sound of flapping once he got airborne and it was gone within four to five-seconds."

Manuel was later able to secure an interview with the witness:

The witness states that they left the Lollapalooza grounds at approximately 9:30PM They were one of the last attendees to leave, in order to allow the crowds to thin out and make it easier to traverse to the hotel.

The witness and her girlfriend both reported that they were talking and walking when they noticed something fly overhead. At first they paid no attention to it and assumed it was just a large bird. They continued walking for approximately one hundred and fifty yards when they noticed the creature in a clearing in the park. They stated that the creature looked like it was hunched over something when it noticed them and they were able to look at it face to face.

They both agreed that it was about five-seconds later that a group of people came up from behind and also saw the creature. They were all pointing and some were even shouting at it. It was at this point that the creature unfolded its wings and took off into the air. Both witnesses described the wings as *membrane like just like a bat's wings and about seven to ten feet wide from tip to tip. They say the creature shot up into the air with minimal effort and was gone within seconds.*

When asked specific questions meant to misdirect, both witnesses stuck with the story they submitted. Neither tried to embellish and both specifically stated that they were sober and fully aware of their surroundings. Neither witness reported any adverse effects following the encounter or the subsequent days after.

I will admit that I'm somewhat skeptical about this report. The description of the being was almost 'too good.' In other words, they were well-aware of the other sightings and had read the previous reports. I decided to give the witnesses the benefit of doubt, but my 'pessimist radar' was alerted when I read the details of the incident.

I also believe that if this account was totally factual, then the witnesses would have had plenty of opportunity to take a photograph. This is not a slight to Manuel, since he gathered the information as it was presented to him. But my innate sense tells me that there are some issues with this narrative. I would have liked to have corroboration as it pertains to this sighting, since there were supposedly many witnesses watching the being. Unfortunately no one else has come forward.

12

'RED LIGHTS' OVER THE WATER

THE FOLLOWING information was forwarded to me in a pair of emails. This particular sighting offers investigative value since it was within a ten mile radius of four earlier and at least two later incidents in south Chicago:

> "I listened to your appearance on Coast to Coast AM, and heard about the Chicago Phantom. I believe I may have seen it near the Lost Marsh Golf Course, right off Calumet Ave. (I-41) in Whiting, Indiana. (The location is approximately half a mile east of the Illinois / Indiana border).
>
> So this possible sighting happened on Saturday, July 1, 2017, around 10:30PM CT. We were heading home from my sister's house. My wife was driving I was the passenger. The kids were sleeping in the back seat and I was just enjoying the ride home. I was looking out my window and noticed two red lights in an area where there are usually no lights. I even told my wife; "hey, I just saw two red lights." I thought it was a little strange but nothing more. I had no strange feelings, but when I started to think of the two lights, they must have been 10 feet

over the water. The red lights were about a 45 degree angle and close to each other.

We take that route all the time and there is no light pole or anything in that area; just water. I thought it could have been a golf cart, but why would they only be using red lights. That little piece of course has no lighting and the street also doesn't have any lighting. The BP Whiting Refinery (approximately one mile away) is way too far away for what I saw. Basically, the two strange red lights were over the watery part of the golf course. - KG."

The 'red lights' were within one hundred to two hundred feet from the point of observation by the witness; and were close together. Did the witness see the red eyes of one of these humanoids?

Not long after I had posted this report, I received a telephone call and an email from two irate individuals who stated that they were not pleased by what I had been reporting. They accused me of exploiting these winged beings and encouraging others to go and hunt them down. One of these people explained that over the past year, they have been observing at least one of these beings feeding in the waters in North Hammond, Indiana. They stated that they had property near one of these waterways and that this winged being should be protected.

I assured them that I had no reason to hunt down this unknown being, and that my only intention was to learn what it was and where it came from. I don't know if I satisfied their concerns, but these terse allegations had also piqued my interest. This may be an excellent general area for a concentrated investigation, including the other nearby locations where the entity was seen.

Rendition of Lost Marsh sighting by Emily Wayland.

I was able to contact a naturalist, who was also a member of the Indiana Wildlife Federation. She was quite willing to answer my questions. But one of the statements I didn't expect to hear from her was that there have been a few 'unexplained' sightings of unclassified creatures in the waterways of northwest Indiana. One account from 2014 involved the sighting of a tall black winged creature that was described as 'a flying monster.' She discounted the sighting because there was no-known animal that fit that description anywhere; let alone in Indiana.

At this point, I was starting to wonder if there may actually be an unknown creature or cryptid somehow thriving in the waterways in and around the Chicago metro area. I was going to keep an open mind as to what the Phantom was, but I still believed that people were seeing something from beyond our Earth plane.

DURING THE SUMMER OF 2017, the United States was under the spell of the upcoming solar eclipse. This once-in-a-lifetime spectacle would be seen in all its glory by millions of Americans. There were also questions swirling about as to what the solar eclipse would deliver. Could it be a precursor to earthquakes or other natural disasters? I was actually quite amused by the hoopla being spewed by various conspiracy enthusiasts. I suppose it was fitting then, that a Phantom sighting occurred during the event.

On Wednesday, August 23, 2017, UFO Clearinghouse received a report from a witness who had been on Northerly Island observing and photographing the solar eclipse:

"I am a little skeptical of reporting what happened but after reading and researching the sightings that have been happening in Chicago, I am a little more confident that I will not be seen as insane. This happened on August 21, 2017, at approximately 1:15PM (Central Time) and the location is just off of South Linn White Drive on the southern end of Northerly Island in Chicago, Illinois. I was with two of my friends and we were there to watch the eclipse that was going to happen over Chicago at about 1:30PM in the afternoon.

We showed up approximately an hour and a half early to set up equipment to photograph and to observe the eclipse. We were watching and observing as the moon began its transit, when we heard a very loud scream. This sounded like squeaky truck brakes that squeal when you're pressing hard on them. At first we thought that's what it was; maybe a CTA bus or big truck with brakes that needed changing or maintenance. We then heard it again. This time it lasted about three-seconds; whereas the previous sound was brief. I looked up to see a large object flying low over the docks that stick out into Burnham Harbor from across the water. We were on the east side of the island, facing west across the water from the parking lot. You can see the docks that line the harbor on the opposite shore. This object looked like a large black bat, but also had human features, such as pronounced arms and legs.

It was flying along the edge of the docks near the open water and was maybe six or seven feet above the water surface. We saw it fly over most of the docks and then cut a hard left, headed toward Soldier Field. We did see it gain altitude as it went over Campus Drive and then toward Soldier Field.

The entire sighting lasted about a minute and a half from the time we saw it to the time it cut left and went toward the field. All three of us saw it and all three of us were sober and not hallucinating. I am pretty confident that other people saw it because most of the island was filled with people there to see the eclipse. There were also multiple people driving around the museum campus, which is always a very busy spot in the city.

I asked that you please take this sighting seriously as it was very disturbing to us to see this object. It looked like it was something that should not be messed with. It was scary and looked like it could rip somebody to shreds if it wanted to. This creature had to be about six maybe seven feet tall; having to guess because it was in flight when we saw it. The wings were enormous and had to be at least six feet wide when we saw them. You could tell that the wings were catching air because there was a wave motion as this creature glided along.

When it banked to the left it flapped its wings at least three or four times to gain altitude over the drive. It did look like it had a small tail from what we could see and that the feet ended in what look like claws or talons. We did not seen many features of the face as it was flying and might have been looking away from us, but of course we could not tell because we were in absolute shock. I do not know what else to compare it to as it was larger than any birds I've ever seen and that includes many of the eagles that I grew up with in Alaska. In fact this thing put many of them to shame in size.

It might not be of any consequence, but right after the sighting there was a decidedly audible hum that was lingering in the area for about thirty minutes. The hum stopped after about a half-hour because we hung around for at least another hour to observe the eclipse and to see if we could possibly get another view of whatever this thing was.

Well, that is my report. I hope to not sound like a complete imbecile but I do know that what we saw was real flesh and blood and was quite scary as Hell. Thank you for your time and attention to this. I sincerely appreciate it."

Manuel added the following comments:

"Contact was made with the witnesses and an extensive conversation was held. The witness who reported the sighting and her friend; both stated that this creature was solid black and reminded them of the harpies in the movie 'Clash of the Titans.' She did state that it had two arms and two legs and both seem to be tipped with talons. The witness stated that the only lingering effect was a loud hum that was heard by everybody. The witnesses stated that the creature was flapping its wings and that it made a sound that sounded like squeaky brakes. When given the chance to add to the story or embellish it in anyway the witnesses stuck to the original story. It is the investigator's opinions that these witnesses are being genuine and that they did see something and are not hoaxing any of their account."

I'm still having difficulty understanding why these particular witnesses didn't take a photograph. I understand that the equipment that they had was filtered for recording the *sun. But for the amount of time they had available while observing the flying being; why not use their cell phone to take a photograph? I understand the shock and amazement of seeing this unexplained entity, but after a minute or so the realization that it may be important to document this sighting should kick in. I suppose that not every person thinks like an investigator.*

If the witness was correct in her assessment and description of this being, then this may have been an entity unreported before this sighting. This description included talons and a short tail. As well, it was compared to a 'harpie' being from the film; 'Clash of the Titans.' If that is the case, then I hope none of the future witnesses has a up-close encounter with this thing.

ON WEDNESDAY, August 23, 2017, I received an account from a young woman who lives in the vicinity of N. Leavitt St. and W. Le Moyne St. in the Wicker Park neighborhood of Chicago. This frightening encounter seemed somewhat similar to the September 30, 2011, incident:

"I guess I'm reluctant to speak about it because I know what I saw; it's hard to believe that it's real. I'm still feeling pretty uncomfortable. I can provide my number if necessary for you. I am not trying to be difficult, but I am just still shocked by everything.

On Monday, August 21, around 8:20PM (Central Time) I was on a phone call for about forty minutes. I took the call in my bedroom in my apartment. I live on the third-floor and the window in my bedroom overlooks the backyard of the building next to me. To the right of this window, about five to six feet away is the neighbor's roof. It is not close enough for anyone to reach my window unaided. There is no balcony or ladder up to my window as well.

About mid-way through the phone call, out the window, which was to my right, (with the curtain and drapes pulled aside) out of the corner of my eye I saw movement and noticed a change in light in my room. I saw what looked like a human-shaped shadow from the mid-torso up in the window. As soon as I turned to look, the shadow moved unnaturally fast to the left and up out of sight. Its movements gave the impression it was taking off to fly. It looked like it used the wall of my building to jump up and away. The shadow was dark gray, when it moved, its body was large enough to block a substantial amount of light, giving me the impression it was long/tall.

The whole experience had to be less than ten-seconds but left me very unnerved. I had run out of my room, trying to explain what I just saw over the phone. About ten minutes later, I finally felt brave enough to go back to my room and shut the blinds/curtains. I did not see anything unusual at that time. I have not really felt comfortable since.

The next day, the person I had been speaking with, showed me your site, as they had done research into what I had seen. I felt pretty uncomfortable reading those other stories, but could see similarities, and was very reluctant to contact you because I having trouble accepting this as real. But I was encouraged to reach out and am hoping to gain more peace of mind.

I'm curious to know if any of these sightings have been violent or if anything bad has happened to the people? Does that thing make repeat visits, or try to get into buildings? Is there anything I should or shouldn't do if it comes back? Is there any correlation in the sightings? Any ideas on what this is, or what its appearance means? Thank you. - KS."

When I received the initial email from the witness, she was very reluctant to produce any further evidence. Her description of the being was vague since she only saw an outline of the shadowy figure through her window; but her reaction and fear overwhelmed her. In fact, her friend eventually talked her into making a report. She is very torn between what she thought she should believe and what she actually witnessed. She knows what she experienced and how it made her feel. I am attempting to answer her questions the best I can, but this witness is just one of many who are having trouble accepting the possibility that this winged being exist in their midst. I have little doubt that this shadowy figure was one of the Phantom beings.

13

ANOTHER SKEPTIC, TURNED BELIEVER

A NEW EYEWITNESS contacted Tobias Wayland at The Singular Fortean Society on August 22, 2017, to report the sighting of a large, winged creature flying over South Pulaski Road in Chicago at around 4:55PM (Central Time). Here's the account:

"I have been hearing about the, "flying Mothman" for a while now but was skeptical about its existence. I just assumed that someone was playing a joke and that the photos (from 2011) that I saw online were photo-shopped. That was until today.

I was driving down S. Pulaski Rd. at around 4:55PM, right before W. 55th Street (in West Elsdon). I saw it soar right over the Shell gas station! It was really fast and I couldn't get a photo because it disappeared before I got to the light.

I guess you can say that I now am a believer as I saw it with my own two eyes. There really isn't much more than that. I only saw it for about three to four-seconds as it flew by.

The rational part of me thinks that maybe it can be a giant Japanese bat that accidentally got shipped here through cargo or something like this. It honestly looked exactly like it does in *the following photo. And I was only a couple blocks away from where this photo was taken when I saw it. I really don't have any details as I only saw it for a few seconds. It was really fast! It looked EXACTLY like this."*

Ah... another skeptic, turned believer. That was happening a lot in the Chicago area. I suppose it's just common human nature to be skeptical about something you have little or no understanding of or that you haven't seen with your own two eyes. As more and more witnesses would come forward, their expression of astonishment and sudden contradiction of conventional thinking was fascinating to read and hear. After forty plus years of research and investigation, a witness' realization that there really are things in this world that are unexplained, is refreshing and stimulating to me. That is what drives me to continue seeking the truth.

DURING THE LAST week of August 2017, I started receiving reports of a large bat-like humanoid in McCook suburb, flying along the Des Plaines River:

"I received a telephone call from an employee ('LL') who works at a trucking firm along US.66 (Joliet Rd.) near Rt.171 (1st. Ave), in the McCook suburb of Chicago, IL.

He stated that 2 witnesses; one a truck driver from the firm where he works, and the other who was a parcel delivery driver, had reported seeing a large being flying along the Des Plaines River near the Rt. 171 exit coming off I-55 (Stevenson Expressway).

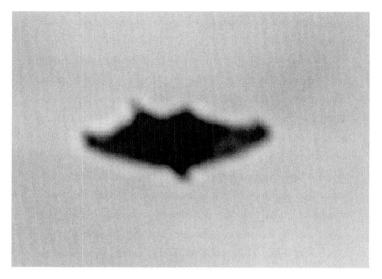

Image referenced; from 8/22/2011 incident.

The first sighting was on Tuesday, August 22, 2017, around 4:30PM CT. The driver told 'LL' what he had witnessed the next day. The flying being was dark brown and black with thick glistening hair on the body. The wings were bat-like, with very long arms and claws attached to the wings. The legs extended from the back and were together. The head was very small, but there was a distinct ridge that ran along the top of the head along the back. The body was quite thin and long, estimated at six to seven feet in length. The wings were very wide and spanned at least ten feet. It was flying along the north bank of the river near the exit overpass, flapping its wings in a slow deliberate motion as it moved downstream. The driver was able to watch it for about twenty-seconds or so after he slowed down.

The driver was not upset, but surprised by what he witnessed. He said it reminded him of a 'small dragon without a tail,' and that this being was larger than any flying creature he had ever seen.

The second sighting was made by a delivery driver, who had witnessed a flying being on Monday, August 28, at approximately 1:15 PM CT. The witness saw a large dark-winged being fly high over the river from the same vantage point as the first driver. The description was of a; "large man with wings" that sailed high above the exit off-ramp at a height of about two hundred feet. The driver observed the being from below and mentioned that it was quickly gliding west, then rapidly ascended into the sky; almost vertically. He told 'LL' that it was the size of a regular man, but with huge wide wings like that of a bat. There were no further details because of the distance.

This witness had mentioned what he had told other employees at his delivery company earlier that day.

It seems that both witnesses were not aware of the sightings in the Chicago metro area. 'LL' contacted me after he Googled "large bats in Chicago" and found my information. He mentioned that he would contact me if he hears of further sightings."

AN INTERESTING ASPECT to these sightings is that I had received a brief report from a woman who had witnessed a flying being at practically the same location as these two sightings. I received the email report from 'JP,' on Wednesday, August 23, around 1:00PM ET. It read:

"Last night around 7PM, we saw what we thought was the biggest bat we've ever seen. It had at least a twelve foot wingspan. Its wings looked like they were attached to hand-

like appendages and they were connected from the fingertips to the feet. It was flying above I-55 near 1st Avenue on the north side of the highway. It was brown with a body similar to a beaver or possum. It was about one hundred feet above us so we're just guessing at the size. All we know is that it was huge. We thought nothing more of it until this morning when I saw an article about a flying humanoid creature that looks like a bat in the Chicago area. We are now certain that the creature we saw last night is the same one in article. We didn't get photos but if you want more info you can call or text us. - JP."

I made several attempts to contact JP, but I never received a call-back or text.

SOON AFTER THE sightings in McCook, I received a telephone call on Tuesday, August 29, 2017, at 5:15PM ET, from a woman; 'NL,' who is a resident of LaGrange Park, a western suburb of Chicago. The witness lives near Possum Hollow Woods, an area where she is an avid bird watcher:

The witness states that at approximately 3:45PM CT on Tuesday, August 29, she was along N. LaGrange Rd. watching the skies above Possum Hollow Woods and Salt Creek. As she looked skyward, she observed what she described as a 'huge flying shadow' glide across the sky at approximately one hundred to one hundred and fifty feet above the trees. Since she is very familiar with the birds in the area, this sighting shocked her. She later referred to the photograph from the Melrose Park sighting, stating that the shape was very similar.

As she continued to watch, she realized that this was an

unknown flying being; and that the wings were broad and rounded in form. As she continued to observe, the winged-being suddenly dipped and descended into a vertical dive at a fantastic speed that the witness could hardly comprehend. As it dove into the trees, hundreds of small birds scattered into the skies. She remained at the location for several more minutes, but the being didn't rise out of the woods. The witness could not walk into the woods from the road since there was a steep bank just beyond the guard rail.

Rendition of McCook sightings by Emily Wayland.

The witness found my contact information and immediately called me; only thirty to forty minutes after her sighting. She was very calm, and stated that she had a 'whimsical' reaction to the sighting; noting that it almost seemed that the winged being wanted her to see it and that it was 'giving her a message' that it knew that she was there watching it. She said that she was set to take a photo, just before the being went into the amazing dive into the woods.

Her description was that the body was six and a half to seven feet in height and that the wing span was ten to twelve feet wide. The wings were rounded like that of an insect with no sharp edges, but were attached along the body. She did not observe any details of a head. She was emphatic that whatever it was, it was 'definitely a living being.' The color was very dark or black. There was no sound.

The witness told me that she intends to keep an eye out in the area of Possum Hollow Woods and the adjacent preserve locations. The witness and I talked twice after her initial call. She is very knowledgeable about Chicago's history and added some insight that may be valuable as we continue to investigate these sightings.

SATURDAY, September 10, 2017, turned out to be a busy day for Manuel and myself. UFO Clearinghouse received a report from a September 7, 2017, sighting in the Lincoln Park Zoo. Then later I received two telephone calls within an hour of each other:

"I took my family out to the Lincoln Park Zoo on Thursday, September 7, 2017, at about 4PM CT. We stayed there until around 7 PM CT and we were just enjoying being outside in

the perfect weather. After the zoo closed at about 5PM CT we stayed, played ball and enjoyed the afternoon.

As we were leaving to head home, we heard a commotion coming from a group of people about 20 yards from us. We looked in the general direction of the commotion and saw people pointing up toward the sky. We looked up to see a large creature with a giant set of wings flying over us, barely skimming the tree tops. We saw it for about five-seconds, as it circled around the trees and then disappeared; heading in the general direction of North Avenue Beach.

Rendition of Possum Hollow sighting by Emily Wayland.

It looked human-like, but had a large pair of wings which must have been at least twelve feet wide, if I had to go make a guess, and looked a lot like bat wings. It was solid black, no discernible features, but you could tell that it had arms, legs and a head, although they looked very skinny. It was flapping its wings repeatedly and appeared to be gaining speed.

After it disappeared, someone in the crowd said that there had been multiple sightings of this thing all summer long. That is why I got online and started looking up these sightings and reported it to your website. I do want to note that when the commotion started and for a few minutes afterwards; many of the animals in the zoo were clearly disturbed and vocalizing as if something had upset them.

There was no further sighting or strange occurrences for rest of the night and we ended up going home."

The overall Lincoln Park section of the city has been a hotspot for sightings throughout this ordeal. I contacted the zoo the next day, but no one wanted to comment about the sighting or if there had been any previous incidents. That same day I received information from two witnesses:

The first sighting was at approximately 11AM CT today (Sunday, September 10, 2017). The witness 'RC' stated that he and a friend were near the intersection of S. Greenwood Ave. and E. 78th St. in Avalon Park in Chicago. As he looked up, he observed a dark object slowing flying across the sky in a northern direction. At first he thought it may have been a jet, but realized that it was moving too slow and that the wings were not that of an aircraft.

After watching the gliding object, he determined that it was a human-shaped being with wings that resembled those of a large bat. There was no sound. He was not aware of the previous sightings, and was given my contact information by another person. I was contacted about an hour after his sighting.

A few minutes after I got off the telephone with RC, I received another call:

At approximately 12:00PM noon CT today (Sunday, September 10, 2017), a military veteran with aircraft flight experience, was in the area of S. Martin Luther King Dr. and E. 35th St. in the Douglas neighborhood of Chicago. She contacted a friend, who then called me with the description that this witness had given them. An unknown being was slowly gliding across the sky with its wings spread. She stated that the wings were shaped like those of a huge bat and that the body was dark and smooth in texture. She also stated that it was not an aircraft or drone because it would not have been able to maintain altitude at such a slow speed. It appeared to be a living being.

The two sightings were about one hour apart and at a distance of 5.42 miles between them. Was this the same winged being? The witness information seemed to suggest that if it was, then this being was flying from a point south of the city towards downtown.

I will also note that this second sighting occurred in an area that was between Guaranteed Rate Field, where the Chicago White Sox were soon starting a game, and Soldier Field, where the Chicago Bears were scheduled to play the first game of the season at 1:00PM CT. I don't know if there was any significance to this, but it is an interesting fact.

THE NEXT DAY, on Monday, September 11, 2017, I received a telephone call from a witness near the lake front, who stated that they were reporting a sighting that had just occurred and that this wasn't the first time that they had seen this winged being:

I received a telephone call today (Monday, September 11, 2017) at 11:39AM ET from a witness; 'PM,' who states that she observed a "huge winged object" at 10:25AM CT (15 minutes prior to the telephone call). This was the second time that she has seen this winged object (previously seen in May). The witness lives on the 25th floor of a high-rise building at E. 47th St. and S. Lake Park Ave. in the Kenwood community in the southside of Chicago.

The witness told me that she saw a huge bat-like being circling above and along the tall buildings located on S. Lake Park Ave. and then out toward the lake. She states that she frequently observes airplanes from her home, but that this object was definitely not a fixed winged aircraft. As well, she has never seen a bird as large as this being. She described it having a six to seven foot human-like body that was dark brown in color, with wide black triangular-like shaped wings that closely resembled those of a bat and spanned at least twelve feet. She mentioned that the wings moved occasionally when it gained altitude.

The winged being eventually flew north towards downtown.

I asked if she attempted to take a photograph. Her response was that when she was watching the flying humanoid, she had an 'overwhelming creepiness' envelope her. She wasn't paralyzed or unable to move, but was shocked and transfixed by what she was observing and never had a notion of taking a photograph.

When I talked to the witness, it was obvious that she was shaken by the incident and exhibited nervousness in her voice; though she was very well-spoken and forthright. She stated that when she looked below from her apartment, she noticed people on the street looking toward the being and pointing it out to others. Other residents in her building have also seen this flying being in the past, having commented to each other and to the witness. The witness will be letting others know that I would like them to contact me and to forward any photographs.

Then the witness commented on some other odd occurrences that she witnessed on the lake. She stated that she and her husband frequently jog on the trails along the lake front together. On at least two occasions, they have observed an unknown creature or being emerging from the water; once near the lake shore along the rocks and at another time out a bit further from the shore. She described it as 'reptile-like,' but was not able to give much detail since most of the body stayed submerged. I asked if it was possible that it may have been the same winged being emerging from the water. Her response was that she wasn't sure.

The Task Force has discussed the fact that many of the sightings occurred near water, but we weren't sure how or if there was a connection. Was it possible that these winged beings somehow inhabited the lake or other water sources? This was another angle to this mystery that needed to be considered.

14

WHAT THE HELL ARE THESE THINGS?

BY THIS TIME, our investigation was into its sixth month. More and more, the prevailing question was; "What the hell are these things?" As far as identifying what the winged beings could be, we just didn't have much to work with. I contacted previous witnesses in an attempt to cover all the bases. Maybe I had missed an important detail somewhere.

It became obvious that it was time to go 'Fortean,' by digging deep through my database and other available sources in an attempt to match up descriptions and behaviors. Perhaps archival and traditional evidence research would provide a better footing for the investigation. But in the back of our minds, we were clearly hopeful that someone would eventually capture a perceptible photograph or video of the Phantom.

There were a few historical flying cryptids, besides the Mothman, that may furnish us some clues.

The first to come to mind was the Ahool. The Ahool is a flying cryptid, comparable to a giant bat, or by other accounts, a living pterosaur or flying primate. Named for its distinctive call; "a-hooool," it is said to live in the rainforests of Java. It is described as having a monkey/ape-like head with large dark eyes, large claws on its short forearms, and a body covered in medium to dark fur. One feature that compares it to the Chicago sightings is that it is said to have a wingspan of ten feet. This is almost twice as long as the largest known bat in the world, the common flying fox.

I received two reports in 2009, from Lee County, Florida, that had characteristics similar to the Phantom and the Ahool:

"I recently had an encounter with a bird-like creature, but I know it wasn't a bird. It looked to be a flying person. I know it sounds weird and crazy but I know what I saw.

Here's the whole story:

On Feb, 5 around 11:30PM my older sister and her husband were taking me, my little sister, my mom and my two nieces to eat at Denny's in a nearby town (Fort Myers, FL). Well, as we were driving on I-75 out of nowhere through the windshield I see a person with wings fly over our car. It went over two times back and forth. I got a good look. It looked like a person with wings. But then again, it also looked like a pterodactyl without a bill. My brother-in-law also saw it and agreed with me. He says it was not a bird!"

Not long afterwards, I received another report from Lee County, Florida:

"I witnessed a person-like creature. I was walking with my girlfriend to her house late at night and by her neighbor's house there are some trees. I saw a person / figure standing in the trees looking at me. I asked my girlfriend if she also saw it. She said that it's always there. I then started to walk closer to get a better view of it, when the creature jumped off the tree onto my girlfriend's neighbor's fence causing it to make a rattling noise. The dogs started barking and then the creature flew off.

We ran into my girlfriend's house; scared it would come back. This encounter happened in Lehigh Acres, FL. I have no clue as to what it was. It was five to six foot tall and had wings like a huge bat. The wings must have been twelve feet or more. The head looked like a flying dinosaur, but there was no beak. There was something that extended from the back of its head. It was very bizarre."

ANOTHER HISTORICAL FLYING CRYPTID / humanoid would be the 'Owlman of Mawnan,' which is a village in southern Cornwall, UK. During the 1976 Easter weekend, two young women saw a "huge great thing with feathers, like a big man with flapping wings," hovering over the church tower at Mawnan. The women were so frightened that their family holiday was cut short by three days.

In another sighting, two people saw it standing in a large tree, near the Mawnan church. At first the witnesses thought someone was playing a trick on them by being dressed in a costume. But as they observed the creature, it flew up into the air, and away from the area. After it flew away, there was a crackling or static noise heard in the trees for some time. One of the witnesses stated, "It stood like a man and then it flew up through the trees. It is as big as a man. Its eyes are red and shine brightly."

In a 1996 sighting, a woman reported seeing a strange glowing light floating over the church. She watched as the light faded away, only to be replaced by another one a short distance away. The color of the lights was orange-red.

In 2003, two teenage girls were out after midnight driving in a vehicle, when they wanted to listen to some music. They wanted to have the music playing loudly, so not wanting to disturb the local neighbors. They drove to the Mawnan church, which is isolated and empty at night. After they were at the church for a few minutes, the girls observed a glowing or pulsating colored light hovering over the church. After a while it vanished and the girls returned home.

In September of 2009, a 12 year old girl named Jessica Wilkins or Jessica Wilkinson encountered the 'Owlman of Mawnan.'

The creature has been described as a monstrous winged creature resembling a mix of three beings; an owl, a bear, and a man. The creature's height is estimated to be seven feet tall. It has large flapping wings that are covered with grayish-brown feathers. The legs and body are also covered with feathers. The eyes are large, slanted and glow bright red. On top of its head are small pointy ears and its feet have large, black talons.

There has been a theory concerning the Owlman of Mawnan that may have some connection to the Chicago sightings. Cryptozoologist Jonathan Downes, of the Centre for Fortean Zoology, maintains that many cryptid phenomena, including the Owlman of Mawnan, result from complex psychosocial and sociological phenomena, and suggests that to classify all such phenomena as 'paranormal' in origin is counterproductive.

Thought-forms may be understood as a 'psycho-spiritual' complex of energy or consciousness, manifested either consciously or unconsciously, by an individual or a group. Thought-forms are understood differently and take on different forms. Paranormal entities and anomalies have been known to manifest from minds of the victims, based on current physical and social conditions. These thought-forms are the prime element of Poltergeist manifestations.

I have considered the 'thought-form' theory as a possible explanation for at least some of the Chicago Phantom sightings.

A few of the witnesses were aware of the sightings before they 'witnessed' the winged being for themselves. I believe that it may be conceivable that some of the later individual eyewitnesses may have unconsciously manifested some of these beings as a psycho-spiritual entity that would only be visible to them. Some people would believe that the thought-form theory isn't that much different from the inter-dimensional or alternate reality hypothesis, since both would demand a manifestation of a being. Even though I have stated that I believe inter-dimensional materialization may be occurring, I still believe that most, if not all, of these winged beings are flesh and blood entities. The thought-form theory can be valid only if the correct conditions are present. Needless to say, this has been an extraordinary phenomenon in which both concepts may come into play.

―――――

WHEN THE CHICAGO Phantom sightings started to increase in number, in the back of my mind I was wondering if these winged beings may be related to another 'Phantom?' This would be a winged-being that I and several other witnesses have encountered along the Conewago Creek in south central Pennsylvania since the late 1980s.

In early autumn 1988, I was at a local exhibition near Baltimore and bumped into Andy, an old friend who was there as part of a group from the Boy Scouts of York-Adams Area Council (Pa.). Both of us had been Boy Scouts together and I was happy to see that he continued as a troop leader. We decided to grab a bite to eat and catch up a bit; it had been twelve years since we had last seen each other. After a while, the subject of my paranormal investigations came into the conversation. He had always been fascinated with ghost sightings at Gettysburg and the surrounding area and had camped near the battlefield on several occasions.

Andy stated that a few of the local troops had recently been camping at the old Camp Conewago and some of the boys had reported hearing "crying" sounds and were spooked bad enough that a few left their campsites early. He stated that he and another scout leader were going to check out the area the following weekend and he wanted to know if I'd at least go up for the day and investigate with them. I accepted the invitation.

I met with Andy and his friend John the following Friday at the campground. They talked me into staying for the weekend, so we soon trekked in the woods to finding a decent camping spot. We setup our tents, and were done by around 7PM that evening. The first night was fairly uneventful, though I sensed that something was watching us. I didn't say anything but kept my eyes open and head clear.

Mawnan 'Bird-man' witnessed by June Melling 17 April (Easter Saturday) 76; (based on a sketch made by her the same day: DS/RJMR).

Birdman monster. Seen on 3rd July, quite late at night but not quite dark. Red eyes. Black mouth. It was very big with great big wings and black claws. Feathers grey.
B. Perry 4th July 1976.

Provided by Jonathan Downes; 'The Owlman
and Others. ' CFZ Communications, 2001.

The next morning was sunny and cool; a perfect day to explore the woods. We sat down to breakfast when John asked if we had heard footsteps and movement during the night. Andy said he slept straight through the night. I mention that I had heard some movement but assumed it was one of my companions. Nothing seemed to be disturbed in the campsite, so we dismissed it. We spent the day walking for several miles through the area. About 6PM we got back to camp and sat down to talk about any little thing that came into our heads.

Later that evening, we were sitting around the fire engaged in a conversation when suddenly a scream rang out downstream from our location. I thought it sounded like an owl at first, but a few minutes later it happened again and it distinctively sounded like a child. I couldn't tell how far away it was but it lasted for several seconds and seemed to fade in and out. We got up and walked a few yards into the woods expecting to hear the sound again. It was quiet for about an hour and we were discussing what could have naturally caused that sound. I have heard bobcats, owls and rabbits scream and none sounded close to this. We agreed that it was definitely the cries of a child.

We decided to stay up for the entire night. There was a full moon and much of the woods and creek were visible. At approximately 1:00 AM, I was walking the perimeter of our camp when I suddenly felt like something was watching me. I stood still and tried to gauge what was going on. I told Andy and John what I felt and we started to walk deeper into the woods towards the fork. We walked about fifty feet when, without warning, we recognized to our right a large dark figure with bright red eyes standing in the creek; and suddenly it shot straight up into the air with an audible "whoosh." A few seconds later, we heard another scream that seemed to fade as if was moving away from us.

We hurried back to the campsite and compared thoughts about this phantom. Andy was shook up and didn't talk for several minutes until I prodded him for his recollection. John was surprising calm and estimated that it stood six foot or so, dark in color and seemed to have something extending from its back. I also noticed the structures on the back and commented that it reminded me of wings but I was unsure. We all agreed that it had bright red eyes. This creature jettisoned so fast that we didn't even have time to get a flashlight on it.

Andy wanted to spend the night in the administration building and come back and collect our gear in the morning. He and John walked back, but I decided to stay in the campsite for the remainder of the night. Nothing significant occurred, though that feeling of being watched remained.

After the investigation and further research, I concluded that this creature or phantom was more than a simple spirit or energy. I was aware of the numerous sightings of a "Mothman" in West Virginia and it seemed that this being was somewhat similar in description. I and other researchers have investigated this area since our sighting and have come up with minimal evidence, though a report of a dark creature was made by a resident who lived near Dick's Dam a few years later.

THEN IN 2008, I received an email from a man who lived a mile or so upstream from this incident (near Dick's Dam). He stated that he had heard similar screams for many years and that the frightful sounds continued to this day. A scout leader also emailed me at approximately the same time and wanted to tell me that a few of the boys in his troop had witnessed what they described as a 'dragon' that was six foot tall with wings and a tail; but looked like it had fur or feathers. He said that the boys seemed serious but he thought they were 'showing off' and dismissed their claims, that's until he read the account of my experience. Since my encounter, almost thirty years ago, I still have no idea what that winged being was. At the time, I dubbed it the 'Conewago Phantom,' though the locals now refer to it as; "Ole Red Eyes." The last reported sighting was on April 29, 2012:

> "I saw a flying 'something' during the evening of April 29 around 7:50PM as I was driving north on Harmony Grove, Rd near the Conewago Creek crossing. I noticed something fly straight up into the air from behind the trees on the creek bank. It shot straight up to the tree tops and spread its wings, then flew east towards Pinchot State Park. It was not a bird; just too

big. I don't know what it was but I'd say it was about 10ft high and had wings like a bat. I didn't notice a head or tail. It was black in color. No feathers. I searched Google and your story came up. I didn't know about the Conewago Phantom sightings. I don't know if it was that thing. I did find something like a large bird seen north of York back in 2006. I found some photos on Google Maps of where this thing was seen by me. Any idea what it was? Thanks. Jim S. - Dover, Pa."

I have recorded a total of six encounters along the Conewago Creek in a thirty plus year period. There has never been a photograph provided. So far, 'Ole Red Eyes' has kept his identity secret.

THE SOUTH CENTRAL region of Pennsylvania has been the scene of other unexplained winged humanoid sightings and encounters. I received an account from a witness who had a bizarre encounter, along with his family, just a few miles south of my home in Hanover, PA:

"My wife, three daughters and I were driving down a dark road in Littlestown, PA about 10 o'clock at night. My wife was driving. I was in the front passenger seat and my three daughters were in the back of the minivan. We were coming around the turn and my wife and two of my daughters screamed out and said they saw a human-size butterfly passed in front of the minivan. It flew about twenty feet in front of the minivan and straight across the road and then disappeared. They said it looked like giant butterfly wings with no head and it was moving very fast. I didn't see it because I was looking out the side window. This just happened a few days ago."

I immediately contacted the witnesses by telephone. This encounter occurred on September 23, 2015, at around 10PM on Teeter Rd., southwest of Littlestown, PA., near the Quail Valley Golf Course (approx. 1.3 miles north of the Mason-Dixon Line). The driver (wife) and the two oldest daughters (18 and 13 years old) witnessed the being. It was described as a six-foot human form (no visible head; similar to some 'Mothman' descriptions) with huge butterfly like wings (one of the daughters said the wings look like large angel wings). The wings had no feathers and were covered in skin or other membrane. The color of the body and wings was light in color, described as a pink-white hue. The being quickly flew directly across the road about five feet. above the road surface (well illuminated by the headlights; about ten to fifteen feet in front of the van). The wings did not move or flap. It came from the area of the golf course and moved south across Teeter Rd. into a small patch of woods. I visited the location and later talked to the witnesses in person. It was obvious to me that the encounter shook the witnesses, to the point where their voices were shaking and strongly emphasizing what they had seen. To this day, I have no idea what they observed. On a side note, this location was 11.4 miles southwest of where I encountered the Conewago Phantom.

IN THE SPRING OF 2017, researcher and Chicago Phantom Task Force member Timothy Renner, told me about an encounter he had with an unknown being in the vicinity of Codorus Furnace. This location is in northeastern York County, PA, and a research area for Timothy and his investigative group. On May 15, 2017, I received an account from a witness who lives in the area:

"My name is Sky, and I'm not even sure where to begin, but after stumbling onto your articles about the Conewago Phantom, I had to get in contact with you. The experience that my mom and I had was terrifying and I'm getting goose bumps just thinking of the possibility that what we saw was actually real. We've had a lot of experiences with the paranormal, but this one takes the cake. I've since moved away from York, but we're planning to move back to Pennsylvania, which led me to research hauntings and cryptid sightings in the area. When I searched 'Conewago Phantom', the pictures made my stomach drop. But when I read your descriptions, including the almost human-like crying; well, I'm still kind of in shock.

It's hard to pinpoint an exact date, but I believe it was summertime in 2010. There were two separate instances that neither of us had thought were tied together. We were living in Mt. Wolf at the time, right by the Codorus Furnace (there's a whole other story about the 'woman in white' for another time?). Behind our house were woods and it wasn't uncommon for us to hear foxes or owls or any other animal making noise out there. But there was one night that my mom had called me outside to listen. She described it as a sad, lonely wailing.

We researched endlessly about what could have possibly made that sound, but we always fell short. Just as you described it; the cries faded in and out and eventually lingered away. I hadn't thought much on it, considering that the actual sighting was the forefront of my memories there. But after reading your description, it makes so much sense.

It was a little bit of time after this happened, when my mom and I were coming home on Codorus Furnace Rd. from running errands. We slowed to a stop, right around Jerusalem School Rd. It was nighttime and we always liked to watch for deer on the horizon of the fields. I was in the passenger seat, trying to see out my mom's window, and that's when I saw this *black form by the back window. I don't even remember what I said or did to get her to look back, but she did.*

She then turned forward, slammed on the gas, and wouldn't even talk to me about it until we got home and in the house. She said that when she turned to look at it, it "stood up" and wing-like appendages spanned out from its back. We both agreed it was massive. I'd say nine to ten feet. I don't recall seeing any red eyes, but it all happened so fast. Personally, I'm more apt to be spooked out by the paranormal, whereas my mom is more curious. But whatever this thing was, it was enough to terrify her. She wanted to go back out to investigate, but I was too afraid to go and she didn't want to go alone.

The next day we returned in the daylight to see if there was a tree or mailbox; or anything else that we confused with what we thought we saw. But there wasn't. Up until now, I jokingly referred to it as my 'Mothman experience,' despite the uneasy undertones. I had no idea this creature even existed. I've told the story to so many, but I think it's hard for them to really grasp what actually happened. To them, I'm sure it just sounds like a spooky ghost story. I've been dying to find an actual explanation to this and I think I finally have.

My grandmother had a similar experience, but she was living in Edgewood, Maryland at the time. She described it exactly the same way; a massive, black, winged figure lingering near her car. She told us that she thought it was a 'fallen angel.'

It's all been very surreal. I didn't think I would ever get answers to what we saw, and it's haunted me to this day. I'm still unsure whether or not this discovery has eased my mind or frightened me even more, but I'd love to talk with you some time. All the best. - Sky."

There have also been a few other general reports, including

an encounter near Lancaster, PA, and a few other sightings along the Conewago Creek. In those instances, the witness information has been sketchy and I have not been able to conduct any interviews.

What are people encountering here in south central Pennsylvania? Can the information from those reports help us in our investigation of the Chicago sightings? Is there an explanation as to why these winged beings are suddenly manifesting in Chicagoland?

In paranormal circles, Chicago has a reputation for retaining a great deal of supernatural and bizarre activity. That in itself may be an element as to why these winged being sightings are occurring.

I know for a fact that negativity can breed malevolent and out-of-control entities. Is it possible that the Chicago area is part of a 'perfect storm' of negative energy and dark spirits, able to manifest or summon unknown beings and other cryptids?

The year (2016) prior to the group of Phantom sightings was the deadliest in Chicago in two decades. The city has been in the midst of a financial meltdown. Too many hopeless citizens are homeless or live in squalor. The drug cartels control over 100,000 gang members in the metro area. Political corruption continues to run rampant. There's dysfunction and chaos. There's contempt and despair. There's cruelty and death. Are we witnessing the vessel of rancor about to burst at its seams?

Many cryptid enthusiasts grew up reading he works of H.P. Lovecraft, and the Cthulhu narrative is his nightmarish legacy. In the narratives Lovecraft wrote, "The old ones were sleeping in the bottomless depths of the oceans until the time when the right astral alignment will awaken them and they will once again walk the Earth, reigning over an unspeakable kingdom of darkness. Their return is awaited by a priesthood of bat-winged humanoids who bide their time concealed by darkness in the unknown recesses of the earth's forgotten caves." Lovecraft tailored many of his works from ancient legends.

In the 'Book of the Jaguar Priests' or 'The Book of Chilam Balam of Chumayel,' it is written that, "The road from the stars will descend from the sky and the 13 Gods of Heaven and 9 Gods of Hell will come to earth." The Maya believed that the end was the beginning and the beginning the end; in destruction would come creation and creation destruction. It would happen at the black hole.

"At the crossroads an image would appear in the sky. The dark kingdom of Xibalba ('place of fear') would manifest itself upon the earth. Xibalba is inhabited by winged creatures with the body of men and the heads and wings of bats. These creatures are blood drinkers and hostile to man."

I started to research various sources and discovered interesting information concerning ancient and modern sightings of bird-like humanoids throughout Mesoamerica.

Around 100 BC, a peculiar religious cult grew up among the Zapotec Indians of Oaxaca, Mexico. The cult venerated an anthropomorphic monster with the head of a bat, an animal associated with night, death, and sacrifice. The monster soon found its way into the holy rituals of the Quiché, a tribe of Maya who made their home in the jungles of what is now Guatemala. The Quiché identified the bat-deity with their god Zotzilaha Chamalcan, the god that controlled fire.

Popol Vuh, a Mayan sacred book, identifies Zotzilaha as not a god, but a cavern ('The House of Bats'). Zotzilaha was home to a type of bat called Camazotz, which has been translated as; 'death bat.' An entirely different story appears in another chapter of Popol Vuh. Here a demon called Camalotz, or

'Sudden Bloodletter,' a single entity, is identified as one of four animal demons which slew the impious first race of men.

In Latin American, it seems that the ancient belief in the 'death bat' still survives into the present day. For example, legends of the winged 'Black-man' (hʔik'al), a kidnapper and rapist, still circulate among the Zotzil people of Chiapas, Mexico. Other bat-demons include the Soucouyant of Trinidad and the 'Tin Tin' of Ecuador. Yet another similar creature appears in the folklore of rural Peru and Chile; the 'Chonchon,' which is a vampire-type winged monster. Is it possible that a natural species inspired the existence of these 'demon bats?'

Several stories supporting the idea of a large bat-like creature have come out of Latin America in the last century. Some believe initial suspects were the common vampire bat species, due to the large size and habit of attacking prey around the head or neck. A 1947 report of a creature presumed to have been a living pterosaur may in fact have been of a large bat. A witness saw five "birds" with a wingspan of about twelve feet as well as brown, featherless, and beaked.

There is another bat-like monster told by a Brazilian couple, the Reals. One night in the early 1950s, they were walking through a forest outside of Pelotas, Brazil, when they saw two large birds in a tree, both of which were reported as winged humanoids.

In March 1975, a series of animal mutilations plagued the countryside near the Puerto Rican town of Moca. During the incident a man named Juan Muñiz Feliciano claimed that he was attacked by a tall, large gray-feathered creature. These bird-like creatures were seen numerous times during the outbreak.

In the mid-1970s, a number of sightings of large man-like birds or bats surfaced in Rio Grande Valley, Texas. The first report came from the town of San Benito, where three people each reported an encounter with a large bald-headed winged creature that made; "tch-tch-tch" sounds.

Then on New Year's Day 1976, two girls near Harlingen observed a large, bird-like creature with a "gorilla-like" face, a bald head, and a short beak. The next day, a number of three-toed tracks were found in the field where the creature had stood. On January 14, Armando Grimaldo said he was attacked by the creature at Raymondville. He said it was black, with a monkey's face and large eyes. Further reports surfaced from Laredo and Olmito, with a final sighting reported from Eagle Pass on January 21.

These few reports are simply scratching the surface of winged human-like beings in Latin America. So how are these encounters related to the winged beings described as the 'Mothman' from West Virginia or large flying humanoids in Chicago?

I have long believed that the Mothman, and other unknown winged beings, are extra-dimensional life forms; that can be summoned by high-energy incorporeal entities that reside on our Earth plane. I believe that these life forms are used in a variety of ways, which includes deployment as a sentry or watcher. There is also some suspicion that these winged beings could have been urged to appear by those who adhere to the occult. Is it possible that these winged beings concentrated in the Chicago area because they were summoned somehow?

There is a fairly recent theory known as the 'Many Inter-acting Worlds' hypothesis (MIW). This profound theory suggests not only that parallel worlds exist, but that they interact with our world on the quantum level and are thus detectable. The theory may help to finally explain some of the bizarre consequences inherent in quantum mechanics. Imagine that the manifestation of unknown beings and certain cryptids in our Earth plane may fit into the criteria as extra-dimensional travelers. I believe the theory is more than speculation and is a rational explanation for many of the cryptid sightings reported worldwide.

NOT LONG AFTER my May 2015, appearance on *Coast to Coast AM*, I received an interesting email from a witness asking for an explanation of an anomalous incident that he had observed:

"*This happened to me one day when I was 10 or so. Both my parents left for work early in the morning. It was a school day and my brother and I were already up and dressed, just waiting around until it was time to head off to school. He was two years older, so he left before me to catch his bus. I didn't have to leave for another hour or so and I just walked to school nearby. He left and it's just me there now.*

About five minutes later I'm on the couch just watching TV, and from our guest bathroom by the living room I hear the toilet flush on its own. It was a loud toilet any ways, and never really worked right so it was easy to hear. I was kind of startled because I thought someone had sneaked into our house, maybe through a back bedroom window. I quickly jumped up and grabbed this crystal dove candle holder as a weapon just in case this person walked out before I could get out of the house. I start running towards the door and as I go past the bathroom I looked. I noticed the bathroom door was three quarters shut so I couldn't see who was in there.

This is where it gets weird. Something made me feel like I had to turn back and see what or who was in there. I knew I could still get away if they opened the bathroom door and came walking out; I'd just take off out the door. So I walked up to it kind of slowly. This is all happening in a few seconds from the first flush and I can still hear the toilet water running. So I kick the bathroom door open with my foot and nobody is in there. I looked up and right above my head I see this tiny golf ball sized circle of bright light appear. It soon grew to the size of a soccer ball. I now think it may have been some type of portal, wormhole, vortex or whatever you want to call it.

I'm right in front of it and staring right into it; point-blank and dead on center. I'm looking into this circle with a hole of bright light and I see this little speck of black moving through it. The speck was getting bigger and bigger, and when looking into this light hole it's got like a curvy road type angle to it. The black speck is now growing larger and getting closer. It was traveling through this hole but I still couldn't make out what it was.

The black speck finally got large enough to where I really got a good look at what it was. It looked like a big black moth about the size of a bat or bird, and it had red eyes. There were also a bunch of sharp little teeth. I was staring at it 2 feet in front of my face. When it reached the front of the hole it quickly swooped out in the direction of my face. I ducked my head and put my arm up to block it but I didn't feel anything brush off my arm. I again looked up at the hole and the bat-like moth wasn't there and the hole of light was now closing up. It was about the size of a tennis ball and getting smaller. It eventually closed up and disappeared.

At that point I ran out of the house and got the hell out of there. I told my brother, mom and dad what I saw when I got home but nobody believed me. For about a week or two afterwards I was kind of afraid to be in there by myself. I'd leave early for school when my brother would leave. But after a couple weeks it all was back to normal.

-Jimmy."

The witness didn't provide a location, though I believe it occurred somewhere in the Southwest United States.

I RECEIVED a similar oral account several years earlier from a couple in northeastern Utah, approximately four miles from the infamous Skinwalker Ranch near Ballard. In that instance, a rancher and his wife had noticed a brightly lit white orb in the yard near the barn. They described it as hovering just above the ground and that it was at least two foot in diameter. It started to shake violently, when a dark figure formed and grew larger. They described it as a huge dark moth that shot out of the orb and quickly flew towards the west. They never saw it again and the orb simply vanished. Did these witnesses encounter a portal? Does the moth shape have any significance? I suppose some people may think that this could possibly be the inception of a 'Mothman' or other flying cryptid.

The fact that this incident occurred near the Skinwalker Ranch may help to explain the possibility of a portal. There have been bizarre reports involving large wolf-like beings, unknown black faceless creatures and glowing orbs coming through a vortex-like aberration that resembled a tornado.

The Ranch is encompassed within a 480-acre area of land that the Ute native people have named the "path of the Skin-walker." Members of the tribe are prohibited from entering this area. It is believed the Navajos put a curse on the land thousands of years ago and it is plagued with Skinwalkers (vengeful shape-shifting witches). This may or may not explain the unexplained activity at the Ranch but, to me, it seems to be more than just a coincidence.

IN AUGUST 2010, one of my Finnish readers, Tapio Mäkinen, alerted me to an expedition to the Waldviertel region of Austria in search of the 'Alp.' He stated:

"For you who not are familiar with the Alp it's an ancient creature. It's described in old books and art like 'Nachtmahr' ("Nightmare") by Johann Heinrich Füssli (1802). It was first mentioned in the 16th century and most of the myths about this creature were made up during the 19th century.

The Alp is a sort of huge bat with humanoid features with longer legs and arms. Since there are no clear pictures of this creature one has to rely on eyewitnesses when it comes to its appearance.

It's covered in fur and is believed to be closely related to flying foxes. The humanoid features are hard to explain but it might be a misunderstanding (it has arms). Most likely it's a thicker part of the humerus and radius bone that might look like arms.

The size of the Alp is disputed and there is a misconception that they are the same size as a full grown man. There is no evidence that this would be the case, quite the opposite. The proportion between the body and the wings are 1:5 or 1:6. An Alp the same size as a full grown man would need a wingspan of about ten meters to fly. This has never been recorded. The wingspan is more likely four to five meters and this would give it a length of about one meter.

There are many differences between a flying fox and an Alp but this is the closest relative. The wingspan of a flying fox is just under 2 meters, so the Alp is bigger.

The myth about the Alp being a vampyre originates from the myths about vampyre bats. There are bloodsucking bats but they are very rare. It was during the 19th century the myths about the Alp as a vampire began. There were no records of the Alp being a bloodsucker before 1817. The myths about vampyres from the 18th century through the beginning of the 19th century incorporate other creatures and present them as vampires. There are also myths about the Alp being a shapeshifter and haunt its victims by entering their mind and giving them nightmares.

My extensive research shows that the Alp is a distant relative to the flying fox. It's extremely shy and has a very long lifespan. There are creatures that can reach almost two hundred years. The explanation that the remains of a dead Alp have never been found is that it's a very small population. They live long and in isolated areas. Where they breed, how they nest and other question remains unknown."

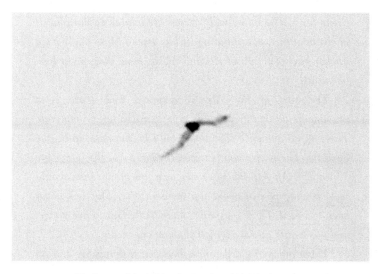

Tapio provided this photo of an 'Alp' in Austria.

THE PHILIPPINES HAS a variety of legendary beings, including a few that are winged. The blood-thirsty Aswang is said to possess wings in certain instances. But there is also a wing humanoid that is somewhat similar to the Mothman. A Filipino reader, who lives in the United States, submitted the following account:

"In the early sixties, the small suburb of San Juan outside the city of Manila was visited by several UFO sightings, and later what is now referred to as Mothman. I was born and raised in that little suburban town about three miles from where these series of "sightings" took place. When I was about a year and half old, my parents moved to a townhouse apartment in the small hamlet of Little Baguio near San Juan. It's a picturesque Spanish-type suburb with stucco houses with red tile roofs inhabited by the well-to-do, with tended gardens. In between these homes ranch-style and townhouse type apartments were randomly scattered. It was in one of these apartments where the haunting of my father started.

As my mother and uncle faithfully recounted, my father would retire to his study as a writer of books and poems to sit at his typewriter in the fading twilight after dinner. Outside his den, a creek could be seen running the length of the house through a huge jalousie window. One evening, according to their recollection, a distinct hum could be heard.

As my father paused from his typing, he glanced out the fading light of the twilight to behold a nine-foot being standing with a black cape in the shadow of a large tree perched at the edge of the creek. The creature was jet black, with the cape glinting in the starlight like leather. As my father backed away from his desk to observe the creature, he noticed a face take form with red eyes in a mask of menace. The creature had horns like a goat and long face that exuded deep horror.

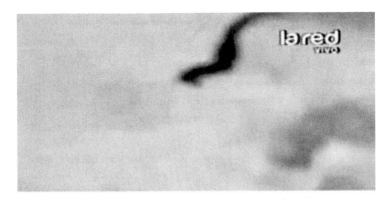

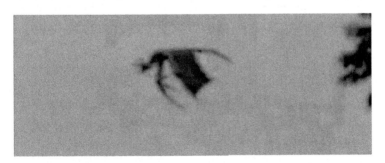

My uncles, who were close to my father, recall the night my father had ran from the room in fear; he had believed he was hallucinating the events, only to find the creature hanging one

night like a bat from the breadth of the expansive den window. It was looking down at him in menace. As they ran to the room, they were overcome by a sense of foreboding and sadness. Upon arrival, the creature had already disappeared, to be replaced by a full moon and the sound the water in the creek.

One night, several months later, my father refused to sleep, fearful the creature would enter his dreams. My mother set up vigil with a live-in servant, a young woman who believed the creature was a demon. As my father finally slept, with my mother sipping tea in the next room, a yell ensued from the maid who had entered my father's den to check on a scratching noise. As my mother rushed into the room, she finally sighted the creature. It hung, bat wings spread, the breath of the window which was about ten to twelve feet in length, glaring pointedly at my mother as she approached.

Fearful but determined to confront the creature, which had haunted her husband, she reached for a cross on the opposite wall and charged the window with it, praying the "Our Father" as she approached.

In the darkness, the creature folded into itself, cloak and all into the ground under the window and disappeared.

The local priest was consulted and blessings were attempted on the apartment and on my father. However, oppressed by the continuous haunting, my father finally committed suicide as a means of escape. That same night, my mother tucked my belongings with me and fled, never returning to the apartment. The creature followed us to my grandmother's house where a priest held mass and blessed the house and all of us. At some point, the sightings of the creature finally stopped (it was only my mother and the maid who saw it) but other ghosts continued to haunt the town; a scene of *much bloodshed in WWII when the Japanese invaded the town.*

That was my first encounter with the unknown. - Anna M."

I have wondered if the high number of winged-being sightings in The Philippines can be attributed to the horrific violence during World War II.

———

AUSTRALIAN JON WYATT, who is a frequent contributor to Phantoms and Monsters, researches many of the available newspaper archives for historical cryptid accounts. Jon found an incredible article published in the Maitland Mercury, NSW, Australia on February 14, 1893:

"A most extraordinary story comes from Joliette, Canada. It is an account of the killing at the little village of Ste Emelie de l'Energie of a monster half bird, half beast, whose classification will puzzle the most deeply learned naturalist. The Enquirer correspondent has the story from the mouth of Mr. Medard Lassalle, a wealthy and reputable farmer of Ste Emelie de l'Energie, whose son, Joseph Lassalle, captured and killed it, and also from three well-known residents of Joliette, where the monster now is being prepared for exhibition to the scientists of McGill University of Montreal.

The story of the capture of the bird-beast and the description is as a follows: For two weeks past the farmers of Ste Emelie de l'Energie and neighboring villages have suffered from the depredation of some beast of prey, who nightly visited their sheepfolds and carried off some of their finest lambs. It was generally supposed that a bear was in the neighborhood, and the farmers have been on the alert for the capture of his bearship.

On Wednesday of last week, Joseph Lassalle, a big young fellow of thirty-five years, went in search of the supposed bear, armed with a double-barrel rifle. Some five miles back in the wood from the village named he was startled by hearing a loud croaking cry, and looking upward he saw, circling high up in the air, an immense creature that he at first took to be a monster eagle.

The bird, or whatever it was, was rapidly descending, and Lassalle, who is a crack marksman, took careful aim and fired. The monster was struck and badly wounded by the heavy rifle bullet, and, screaming with pain and rage, it came tumbling to the earth. As it landed he gave it the other barrel of the rifle, and still thinking it was an eagle, rushed on with his clubbed gun.

A terrible battle ensued, lasting for several moments; then the victory was with the man, and the monster lay dead at this feet. He had now time for a closer inspection of his game, but the thing presented such an awful and unnatural appearance that he was terror-stricken and ran back to the village for help.

He was accompanied (back to the scene) by this father and four other young farmers. The monster was then carefully examined by the farmers, who described it as follows. It had two great wings measuring fifteen feet from tip to tip. The head, which was fifteen inches in circumference, resembled that of a large monkey. The body was five feet long, and, while the back part was covered with big black feathers, the under part was covered with a fur or coarse hair. The feet or claws resembled the legs of a wolf, and under the tail feathers was a long appendage with a tuft at the end that looked like the tail of a large calf. Lying with wings extended on the ground the monster looked as big as a *horse, and when weighed was found to turn the scales at 300 pounds. A team had to be sent for to bring it back to the village."*

This was seen by Mr Alder Charland, a councillor of the town of Joliette, who was going through the country purchasing produce. He bought the monster probably for exhibition purposes from the Lassalles, and Friday evening last it was brought by train to his place of business in Joliette, where it in now in process of preparation to prevent decay, after which it will be shipped to Montreal for scientific examination.

Those who claim to have seen the monster say it is the most extraordinary sight they ever witnessed, and it is hardly possible that all the respectable men who tell this story about it can be lying, and, if not, what can the monster be that is at present causing such a sensation at the Joliette district of the province?"

Did the young farmer kill a Mothman or other winged humanoid? What happened to the alleged flying monster? Well, that seems to be a huge mystery. If M. Charland took it to Montreal for examination it may well have disappeared into the vaults of the scientific establishment to be never seen again. The Smithsonian Institute in Washington, DC has been accused, from time to time by cryptid researchers, of stashing important exhibits that would possibly set the scientific community on fire.

Someone in the Task Force had mentioned that the Chicago occult and spiritual community is widespread and strong. I believe that it is entirely possible, because of the varied cultures and beliefs within the city, that an individual or group may have attempted to evoke a spell or contact a deity. I've seen and read a lot of bizarre phenomenon in my time and there has been an increased trend of unguided mysticism throughout the world. If these winged beings were conjured by the use of Black Magic or another form of sorcery, I wouldn't be too surprised.

There have been many people who have offered a wide array of identifications of these winged anomalies during this investigation. An overwhelming theme has been that these beings are 'demons.' That would imply that these are evil enti-ties, and that they have the ability to possess and torment their victims. I don't particularly care for the word 'demon' since it eventually relates to a disciple of Satan and the underworld; or more precisely, entities invented by the ancient text writers. Everyone is entitled to their own beliefs, but I feel that the early writers used simple explanations for unexplained phenomenon. Another identification that has been offered is that these are 'Fallen Angels,' possibly the beings described in the Book of Enoch. They were known as 'The Watchers,' and that these fallen angels are kept "in everlasting chains under darkness," and are bound "in the valleys of the Earth" until Judgment Day. The Book of Enoch states that these Fallen Angels mated with human women, resulting in offspring known as the Nephilim. These offspring were giants, often with six fingers, six toes, double rows of teeth and massive appetites for blood. Maybe the writer of the Book of Enoch forgot to mention the wings.

Some researchers, including myself, believe that the Watchers in the Book of Enoch may have been an interpretation for alien beings. I'm not saying that everything written was factual, but it can and should be considered for analysis. That being said, is it possible that the Chicago winged humanoids could be a type of extraterrestrial being? I personally don't prescribe to the theory that all UFOs are interstellar modes of transportation for aliens. But there have been a few worldwide accounts that closely relate to winged humanoids.

On August 29, 1967, in Cussac, France, two children saw a sphere-shaped UFO, 2 meters in diameter, and what they referred to as "four little devils" on the ground. One of the humanoid beings was bending over, apparently busy with something on the ground, and another held a mirror-like object. They were observed to levitate before quickly entering the UFO and flying away. The UFO was said to make a soft whistling sound and smelled of sulfur.

These beings were "completely black," but with a shiny look which one of the children compared to that of silk. The children could not be certain whether the color was that of the beings' skin, or of some sort of protective suit, for there was no visible dividing line between any possible clothing and the heads of the beings, which were bare.

The limb proportions were not completely in accordance with the norms of our species. The arms were somewhat too long and thin. The children could not distinguish anything which might serve as hands. The legs were short and thin. The head seemed of normal proportions relative to the body, but the cranium was pointed and the chin equally was very much accentuated. There was no mention of wings, though the beings easily accelerated into the air.

I RECEIVED an interesting account from a witness in the Czech Republic:

> "I live in a town north of Prague in the Czech Republic. My family and I have lived here for many generations. My homeland is full of stories about legends, myths and ghosts. I had never taken these legends seriously until I had an encounter with this unknown 'thing.' I looked on the internet and most of what I found led me to your site 'Phantoms & Monsters.'

My home is near the Vltava River. I can look out from my second floor and observe the entire waterway. The time was close to 10pm and I was sitting on the terrace on the 2nd floor. I noticed a red light floating over the river and it continued for several minutes. I have seen many white and yellow orb UFOs over the river at night, but this was different. I then observed the red light move towards the riverbank in my direction. The light was gaining altitude and moving towards me. When the light started to pass over me, I could tell from the moonlit sky that it was a large bird with huge wings. The entire front of this bird was glowing bright red. There was no sound.

As I watched, it started to circle above me without flapping the wings and was descending towards me. It slowly flew lower until it finally landed on the roadway beside my house, which was about sixty meters from me. The street lamp illuminated the bird enough to where I got a very good look at it.

I can only describe it as a "human bird." I read your stories about the Mothman and these match closely. One difference is the size. This "human bird" was very tall; I would say four meters! The head was very large and red light glowed all around the circumference. It had long legs and a torso like a man. It didn't walk but hopped like a bird. The wings were shaped like those of a flying fox. I watched it hop along the road for several minutes. Then it disappeared; just vanished.

This incident took place in June 2013. I have not heard of other people seeing this "human bird," though I'd be surprised if any of the local people would mention such an experience. - KT."

The Chicago metro area is well-known for consistent UFO reported sightings throughout the year. An interesting angle noticed by the Task Force was that during the time of the

Chicago sightings there was a stark decreased of UFO sighting reports. There is really no explanation for the lack of UFOs, but it is an interesting fact.

HERE IS another incident that occurred near Philadelphia, PA:

"When I was younger my mom, my 2 brothers and myself were walking in the woods. My mom would sometimes take us for walks. We saw what appeared to be a very old man in a black cloak standing next to a green, ground electric box; they are like four foot by four foot square.

When we got near him it turned, looked at us then took off vertically into the sky and then the black cloak appeared as black wings.

Its description is seven feet tall, with pale skin and a human-like physique. It has a very old looking, with black wings that looked like what one would think as a fallen angel. My mom looked up in the sky and there was a triangle craft with three lights hovering for about a minute. It then took off and we never saw the being or the UFO again."

I can go on and on with possible identifications and examples of winged humanoids worldwide. The examples that I have provided demonstrated a variety of possibilities. Needless to say, we were still no closer to determining what people were seeing in Chicago.

15

BLACK DEVIL

IF YOU REMEMBER, on April 16, 2017, in the Hispanic neighborhood of Humboldt Park, an owl-like humanoid standing on two feet had looked directly at several witnesses. The reporting witness referred to this being as a huge 'Lechuza,' except it was about six feet tall and possessed large glowing red eyes.

Then about a week later, several witnesses on the Lower West Side at the Chicago International Produce Market described an encounter with a perched being that was completely black except that it had bright yellowish/reddish eyes like a cat. It stood there for a minute or two staring at everyone before shooting up into the sky and disappearing; resulting in the witnesses feeling very uneasy. It had wings like an owl, only bigger and you could hear it flap those wings when it took off.

Both witnesses referred to this anomaly as a huge owl-like being. So let's move forward to Thursday, September 14, 2017, when the following account was received by Manuel Navarette at UFO Clearinghouse:

"On Monday, September 12, 2017, at about 10:30PM CT I was leaving work and walking down the street toward Millard Avenue in the Little Village neighborhood of Chicago. I stopped at the store to pick up a couple of items that I needed at home and left, turning to my left onto Millard Avenue to walk toward home. As I was walking I saw something that looked like a large person but had huge black wings and a pair of glowing orange eyes. At first, I thought it might be a large owl, but as I got closer I realized that this person was at least seven feet tall. I'm five foot four inches and this thing towered over me. It stood there and looked right at me for about 10 seconds and made a sort of chirping sound as I approached it.

My first thought was that this was the devil and started praying as I walked. I kept walking because I felt that if I stopped I was going to be paralyzed with fear. As I got to about twenty feet from where it was standing it let out a very loud screech that sounded as it was trying to warn me, before leaping up into the air and taking off in the direction of West 25th Street. I watched it disappear into the night and continued saying my prayers as I walked toward home. When I got home I was hysterical and crying and my family came rushing to my side when they saw me crying uncontrollably.

I related the story to everybody in the living room and my grandmother said that it was either the devil or a Lechuza. She stated that either way I was very lucky to make it home and that saying my prayers had protected me from this thing. I slept at night with the window locked, curtains drawn and a light from my desk on. Even though I slept with the lights on I still dreamed of this horrific thing and that it was coming to get me. I pray to God that I never see this thing again and now I know that my prayers protected me from whatever this thing was."

Manuel later stated:

"An investigator for UFOCH talked to the witness early this evening, (09/14/17). The witness reiterated the story as reported. No embellishment of the story was given when presented the opportunity and when asked a series of questions about the sighting, she gave no variation of the original sighting reported. The witness stated that she was still visibly upset by this sighting, even forty-eight hours removed. After speaking with the witness and going over the sighting with her in detail, it is the investigator's opinion that the witness did see something that evening and that her report is credible.

The witness also stated that she has heard stories from the surrounding neighborhood that other witnesses have seen what they describe as "Un Diablo Negro" or a "Black Devil" in the neighborhoods within Little Village. When asked if she could point me in the direction of any other witnesses, she was very hesitant to divulge any information. After some time speaking with her and assuring her that the witnesses could remain anonymous she agreed to refer any witnesses she knew to UFOCH."

Manuel issued a plea to any witnesses that have had similar encounters in the Little Village neighborhood. He also assured that witness identity will remain anonymous if they so wished.

Manuel also pointed out to me that, 'El Diablo Negro,' is very descriptive and what the witnesses see this being as. In particular, Little Village is a heavily Hispanic (mostly Mexican) neighborhood. Many residents are very superstitious, and an encounter like this would be seen as a devil, demon or a witch where almost all of the households are Catholic. But many still practice quite a bit of Curandera (folk healing) and/or Brujeria (witchcraft).

I WROTE EARLIER that Chicago has a well-known history of high strangeness and anomalous encounters. As well, Lake Michigan is not exempt from bizarre activity, especially when it involves humanoids.

On April 8, 1954, Mrs. Lelah H. Stoker of North Sheridan Road had returned to her apartment around 4:30PM from the library. When she looked out her window she observed a very brilliant white, parachute-like object, with a suspended human form skimming over Lake Michigan in all directions, about 1 mile away. She called two neighbors, William Baruszak, a vice-president of Western United Dairy, and his wife. Mr. Baruszak saw a large object floating about one hundred meters off shore, which he took to be an experimental balloon and did not take much notice.

At 16:45PM, Lelah called the Coast Guard, but as the searching seaplane neared the area, the object descended and seemed to condense in size, landing among sporadic foliage along the shoreline. From the object a small, but well-proportioned humanoid figure, dressed in a green one-piece suit, with a tight-fitting headdress disembarked, walked up and down the frontage behind the low stone wall, and blended in with the grass. After the aircraft left, the object re-inflated and hovered over the water. The occupant, who was now suspended in the air, re-entered the craft, which took off at high speed eastwards, without noise. During a tilt, Lelah noticed two parallel bars on the underside of the spherical umbrella.

The incident was investigated by Army Intelligence, and later entered into Project Blue Book.

The Lake Michigan Triangle is a well-known hotspot, noted

for mysterious disappearances of both land and sea craft; similar characteristics of the Bermuda Triangle, including ghost ships, strange disappearances and even UFO sightings. But the city's lake shore offers its own share of unexplained weirdness.

In February 1965, while walking along the Chicago shore of Lake Michigan about sunrise, Harvey Keck saw a saucer about six feet high resting on four-legged landing gear. Near it was a five foot tall "robot or being, stocky in build." The being's skin was tanned, eyes set far apart, and he had a pointed chin. His head was encased in a glass-domed helmet. The incident was reported in the local press the next day.

THE CHICAGO NEWSPAPERS, as well as most other media, had little problem reporting UFOs and unknown beings back in the 1960s. As far as the Chicago Phantom sightings, the media has been a bit more reluctant to get the story out into the public. The city has had its fair share of humanoid encounter accounts before the recent winged being sightings:

Lincoln Park, Chicago, IL – In August 1998, at about 3:00AM, a light came in through the window that early Sunday morning, which woke up the witness. The window was covered almost all the way except for an opening at the very top in which the bright light came through. As the witness wondered what it could be, a being emerged through the covered window like a ghost would go through walls. The witness was frightened until this being told him in his own voice; "don't worry everything going to be ok."

All of a sudden the witness became calm. The being then began to walk around the bed and that's when he realized that he couldn't move his body, only his eyes. He followed the being with his eyes and had the impression that it was a female. This being had long dirty blond hair, big eyes, a slit for a mouth, and two little holes for a nose; its skin was a bluish-greenish color. It stood next to the bed and again in the witness's voice told him that everything was going to be ok. It sat down on the bed, reached over and began to massage the witness's bad knee in which he had problems walking up and down stairs and pain.

The next thing the witness knew; he was waking up, not realizing what had happened over night. He started walking to the bathroom and that's when he realized that the pain was gone. He began to jump up and down very happy when he suddenly remembered the "dream" or event from the night before. The knee pain never returned to this day.

I'm always fascinated by the 'healing encounters,' while hoping one of the less frightening humanoids will find their way to me and do the same. This next one I just don't want any part of.

IN AUGUST 1999, a man, who was visiting a friend in Chicago, was sleeping on the sofa in the living room. He suddenly woke up feeling very panicky and totally unable to move. Looking towards the front door he saw a huge humanoid figure, well over seven feet tall, standing by the door.

The figure resembled a large "praying mantis" and was wearing something resembling a black and purple cloak. Its skin was dark gray in color. It slowly approached the witness and reached out to him with a large hand with long thin fingers and grabbed his shoulder. At this point the witness lost consciousness and does not recall anything else of the incident. He remembered also feeling very cold during the encounter.

That type of encounter is one that you worry about for the rest of your days. I have talked to experiencers who are still concerned about an abduction encounter several decades after the fact.

———

ABOUT FOUR DAYS after we received the Little Village encounter report, a similar winged being was reported across Lake Michigan:

"Hello Lon, I've been scanning the internet trying to find anything that resembles what I saw about one week ago today here in Lansing, Michigan. Your articles on the Chicago bat creature / Owlman / Mothman seem to be the closest I could find. Especially the article titled 'Big Winged Being Observed on Chicago Suburb Home Roof.'

It was about 5:45 AM and I was preparing to leave for work. As usual, I glanced out of my small bathroom window to see if it was raining. It was very calm and dry that morning, but then I noticed an unusual shape on my neighbor's rooftop. Obviously, the sun was not up yet, but it was just bright enough that I could see the outline. I enclosed a picture drawn with Microsoft paint. I do own a cell phone, but it's one of those cheap Consumer Cellular ones, and those are worthless in low light.

I stared at the figure for about thirty-seconds and it never moved. There was tree foliage behind the creature. I'm thinking it may have been sitting (or perched) just on the other side of the roof, as I never saw a head or glowing eyes. It's hard to guess on the size of the being as I only saw the wings. I was about 20 feet away from it. I wished I had stared at it longer or even shined a flashlight on it, but I didn't want to be late for work. - CS."

I asked the witness to provide further details, if possible. He did state that the image he provided was wrong, in reference to the chimney. The being was perched on the other side of the chimney, but the wing was so large that it extended back in front of the chimney and totally obscured the witness' view of the front of the structure. If this is a similar being, as seen in the Chicago area, then it may be originating at another location or flying across Lake Michigan.

Some members of the Task Force, including myself, were interested by the reports of similar winged beings at other locations. It wasn't unusual for me to receive a flying humanoid report every other month or so. But since the time the Chicago sightings started, there has been a steady increase of sightings in other parts of North America.

SOON AFTER THE LANSING, Michigan sighting, another account surfaced in Chicago. But this one was a bit more bizarre than the previous accounts, because this being was moving in an unexplained manner:

"I'm a former Chicagoan and I was on a visit last week. I stayed a night downtown at Sofitel Chicago Magnificent Mile (20 E. Chestnut St). During the early evening, I looked out our window from the 30th floor and saw what I, at the time, assumed was a maintenance man or something in the roof of a shorter building below ours. But, it moved too fluidly and

disappeared too quickly for a man. It was gray in color and the shape I would definitely describe as a male (with no clothes).

I'd say it was about six feet tall. There were no unfurled wings.

It occurred on Sunday, September 10, 2017, at approximately 7PM CT and the thought of it hasn't left me. I couldn't see a door or anything that would allow a person to slip out of sight. It was odd to see someone/something on a roof with no rooftop features like a pool or outdoor seating, and it didn't look like there was any window-washing, construction, etc., that would easily explain why a person was on a high rise roof and then disappeared so quickly.

I told myself it was nothing and forgot about it; but on a whim I called my friend, who'd been with me, and he told me that there have been lots of sightings of humanoids in Chicago.

I immediately panicked a bit, and I have to tell you, I am very scared of things like these. I hope it doesn't mean any harm towards me or anyone else. Luckily, I live in Nashville. Are these things vindictive? I'm a humble tarot reader but I don't want to cause trouble. - AL."

This is a very interesting incident, because the witness was able to see this being move about without flying. The witness later told me that she thought she was 'looking at a ghost because of how fluidly it moved around.' As far as the being disappearing; did it fly away or simply vanish? The witness has no idea how it disappeared. I believe the building roof in which the being was seen was either the Talbot Hotel or Intermix which are across E. Delaware Pl. I attempted to double check with the witness, but it seems was a bit more disturbed by the incident and chose not to reply to my request.

There was a debate among a few members of the Task Force whether this sighting was worthy of noting on the interactive map. I just had a sense that this 'rooftop' humanoid may be of some importance later in the investigation, so I added it.

THE VERY NEXT DAY, a report describing an encounter with a 'skinny gargoyle' was received by me from a truck driver in Florida:

"Hello, I had read about these encounters of bat-like humanoids and obviously thought it was pretty fascinating. I just recently started a new job in Clearwater, Florida where I'm delivering donuts for a major company. I deliver along a route which consists of four different stops. I drive from Clearwater to Port Richey, then to Brooksville and Zephyrhills.

Two weeks ago I had the night off, so another guy worked my route. And in case you don't know Brooksville, Fl and Zephyrhills, Fl. are both riddled with dark roads with no street lights, and just trees to the left and right side of the road. Apparently when he was driving between his third and fourth stop near Zephyrhills, (on Rt. 98 / US 301 at about 3:30PM) he said he saw this "thing" floating stationary about fifteen feet off the ground next to a tree.

As he got closer he realized it looked like a dark-colored humanoid in a cannonball position just floating in the air. He said by the time he asked himself; "WTF is that?" The creature unraveled itself and it spread out its legs and giant bat-like wings. He didn't know what color the creature was but he said it was definitely a dark color and it had human-like legs. And he said at the same moment it spread its wings and legs it flew toward his truck at an unrealistic speed like a fighter jet.

He said he almost crashed the truck in the ditch because

it basically paralyzed him with fear. He said it happened so fast he didn't get a look at the face but he said it was probably between five and six feet tall and dark colored and it had human legs with bat wings. He also said that about a half mile before he saw the creature, he saw a bunch of dead deer on the side of the road. Like piles of deer, two separate piles of at least four deer. He assumes it was eating them. The witness is a pretty soft-spoken dude and intelligent. The way he tells the story, I can tell it really freaked him out. - AP."

I called AP, who recounted the incident that the witness described to him. He told me that the witness told him that the being looked like a 'skinny gargoyle.' The witness was unable to get a good look at the face, so there was no mention of red eyes or other facial features. The legs were definitely human-like and the wings span was at least 12 or more feet in width. AP also stated that while describing the encounter, the witness started to look pale and distressed.

Once again, we have an incident with a similar type of winged being seen at a location far from Chicago. The two piles of dead deer seen along the Florida highway were highly unusual. There had been no remnants of animal kills or attacks reported by any of our witnesses. Up to this point, we had no idea if these beings in the Chicago area were feeding on wildlife or other animals.

THEN ON WEDNESDAY, September 20, 2017, Manuel acquired a disturbing account that occurred approximately two blocks from the previous encounter in Little Village. This time, a pair of siblings witnessed a brief brush with a winged being by a person walking out of a neighborhood corner store. After that, the subsequent events turned out to be frightening:

> "We were walking back from visiting a family member's house, when we saw what looked like a huge bat (later described as having "large wings and black") fly over our heads and continue down the street. As we continued walking, we saw that the bat had landed on the ground across the street from the tiendita (convenience store) on the corner of S. Ridgeway Ave. and W. 24th St. We then noticed that it was looking right at us as we walked toward the intersection, it was very easy to see it with the lights. As we got nearer, we saw someone come out of the tiendita across the street and this thing turned its attention toward the person, who saw it and screamed and took off running. It was then that it turned back to us and opened its wings and took a step toward us. My sister and I did not stand around to see what was going to happen next and took off running back toward W. 23rd St.
>
> The family members' house where we had come from was near the viaduct where the train goes over. This large bat let out a shriek and took off into the air, because it flew just over our heads and then landed about fifteen feet in front of us on the road. It looked right at us and shrieked at us. At that time a car turned onto S. Ridgeway Ave. from behind us on W. 24th St. This bat took off from the road and flew off, leaving us cowering on the sidewalk.
>
> We have never been so scared in all of our lives and we hate to think what would have happened to us if that car had not turned the corner when it did. The car continued its way, not even stopping and we headed back to our family member's house and her son gave us a ride home."

Manuel noted that after he received the report, he made

contact with the witnesses and spoke at length with both of them by telephone. Both siblings spoke of the events leading up to the encounter, neither strayed from the story that they wrote in the sighting report. Even after being questioned by Manuel separately, they both told the exact same story with no embellishment. They then agreed to meet with Manuel to retrace the steps at the location of the encounter at a later date.

Manuel expressed to me that he was a bit disturbed and worried that future sightings may become violent. Besides the aggressiveness of the being, this was the second encounter in the same neighborhood. There had to be a reason why it showed up so close in time to the previous sighting location.

A FEW HOURS after receiving the second report, the third account was sent to Manuel. This time the incident occurred about five blocks west of the previous Little Village locations:

"On September 9, 2017, at about 10:30PM, I was standing outside with some friends, grilling carnitas, drinking beer and listening to some music. We were on S. Harding Ave., just past W. 25th St. in La Villita (the Little Village neighborhood of Chicago). We were talking when we heard a very loud sound, like a scream that was loud enough that the entire neighborhood must have heard it. We looked around to see if someone needed help. One of my friends saw a large black figure with large black wings land across the street near a neighbor's house. It landed right past the tree and was standing by the gate to the adjacent fence. It was easy to see because the fence is white and the streetlight across the street was lighting up the area.

It stood there and it seemed to be doing something with its wings. At one point this thing stretched out its wings, which must have been about 9 feet wide, but did not look like the wings of a bird. The thing stood there for about fifteen-seconds longer before it must have noticed us and then looked right at us with large glowing red eyes. Then it shot up into the air, over the houses and was gone. We all saw it and it looked like a black demon with large wings."

This time, the reporting witness referred to the winged being as a "black demon" with large wings. This report was actually the first sighting in the Little Village neighborhood, though it was reported to us much later.

I had stated earlier in this book that I believe that the flying humanoid phenomenon was the result of a summoning by another entity. This is a theory that I developed based on testimony by other encounter witnesses, in particularly those people who experienced other unexplained activity in the locations where the Mothman of Point Pleasant has been seen.

Some of these witnesses were novice paranormal investigators who had obtained EVP (electronic voice phenomena) evidence in the old West Virginia Ordinance Works during the past decade. Not only did they successfully record voice phenomena, but many were subjected to a spiritual or entity energy attachment that continued for several years. As well, at least one of these witnesses had a close encounter with a Mothman-like being later at another location.

The closely timed group of encounters in a five block radius in Little Village is intriguing. It was apparent that this winged being was there for a reason. Could my theory of summoning be in play for these particular encounters? After a discussion with the Task Force, the general thought was that this concept needed to be examined in more detail.

16

A SEASON OF CHANGE

THE AUTUMN EQUINOX has come and gone, and I had just recorded the 50th Chicago Phantom sighting in 2017. This is the time of the year that the Pennsylvania German folk would refer to as the 'hush before winter.' A time for harvest and reflection; before the Hexerei purveyors would begin to cast spells of obsession, courage, transformation and death. I don't really remember how I felt about those beliefs when I was a young boy, but some of the stories I was told piqued my curiosity.

Autumn was always a season of change for me, because it felt like I was awakening from a long sleep. Even now, it is still my favorite time of the year and not because of football, festivals, etc.; t's much more than that. It's a spiritual cleansing of sorts. But it is also a time to be cautious and mindful of those who intend to cause harm. This year, it's a time of anxiety and onus; waiting to see if the Chicago sightings are a precursor to woe.

I have attempted to dispel any notions of foreboding related to the sightings. But there is always that small bit of perception lingering in the back of my mind, 'was I wrong?' I try not to think about it, but the sentiment is brought up in practically every conversation or interview I am a part of when the discussion turns to the Chicago Phantom sightings. The Little Village encounters have introduced the possibility that witchcraft and the occult may be part of the equation. There are a few members in the Task Force team who are familiar with the rituals of paganism and the use of certain black arts. But many residents in the Little Village community have a variety of spiritual beliefs, combined with religion and the occult. It's difficult to pinpoint any connection to the sightings and the esoteric convictions that are practiced.

This is going to be a matter of finding and recognizing the signs, which involves more boots-on-the-ground. This will be just one piece in the puzzle, albeit, an important piece.

———

A FEW DAYS after the autumn equinox, I received a welcomed letter from a friend and colleague in France. André and I have corresponded to each other for over a decade, mostly on the subject of UFOs and non-terrestrial life-forms. He offered his profound thoughts on the Chicago sightings, gleaned from his extensive research into the unexplained:

> *"What about the Chicago Batman, or Batmen, since the question is have there been several apparitions in different places at the same time or is it a single entity showing up different times in the same neighborhood? The answer to this depends of course on collating witness reports, which is not my concern.*
>
> *I feel certain that the Batman case is somehow similar to that of the Greys. They come into our space-time because it*

offers a unique opportunity for making up thanks to change. The nature of this change is cosmic.

The solar system, which is located at about two-thirds the distance from the center of our galaxy, orbits around the center on a plane which stands at an angle to the median plane of the galaxy. The movement is related to the 25,920-year period of the precession of equinoxes. When our Sun passes exactly through the median plain of the galaxy we have a Transition. This brings about many changes; cataclysms of all sorts, climate changes, and an expected pole inversion. (Even though we are responsible for depletion of natural resources and pollution of the planet, major climate changes are not of our doing but, through misinformation, they serve the interests of the "military industrial complex.")

But Transition modifies not only the physical environment but also the electromagnetic vibrations of life on Earth, of our psyche and spiritual consciousness. Religious persons call this Ascension. To human souls this offers a unique opportunity to accelerate their progress on the chosen course. But it also opens "worm holes" between dimensions facilitating the appearance in our physical space of many forms of life coming from the past or the future. This for instance explains apparitions of pterosaurs, shape-shifting entities and other strange life forms.

Much more important, Transition brings about the end of our civilization. Not in so many centuries, nor even decades, but right now! Any human whose consciousness is not asleep is aware of this. For the same reasons the same happened with previous civilizations, the latest one being Atlantis, where from many short Greys are very likely shipwrecked souls.

This is also the opportunity taken by Christ to reaffirm his teachings, notably also because after two thousand years our knowledge and intellectual capacities are sufficiently developed to understand him. As for the concentration in the

Chicago vicinity, it may be an interesting field of research for scientists of various disciplines. What is the history of this region, the geology, the fauna, human population, etc. from recent to very ancient times? There may be a clue to discover."

I have believed for quite some time that most cryptids were the result of a Space Time Continuum that allows non-terrestrial beings to emerge from another dimension or reality. In the case of the Chicago sightings, there may have been a mechanism used to open a 'worm hole' between our two worlds. Taken in that context, the use of magic or the occult in order to facilitate the 'opening' may not seem too improbable.

I RECEIVED a telephone call on Tuesday, September 26, 2017, at 11:50AM ET from 'ID,' a local Chicago nightclub performer:

He had just gotten off of work and was driving home, westbound on W. Belmont Ave. At 1:15AM CT, he had stopped for the red light at the intersection of W. Belmont Ave and N. Damen Ave in the West Lakeview area. He was the only driver and person at the location. As he waited for the red light to change, he noticed to his left something large was perched on the streetlight pole that extended over N. Damon Ave. As the witnessed looked closer, he recognized an unknown being crouched down on top of the pole. The streetlight above the pole illuminated the being, giving the witness a brief opportunity to obtain an excellent observation.

The witness states that the entity was crouched for about five to ten-seconds. It then stood up on two distinct legs. As it stood, it unfurled its wings and quickly ascended into the night sky.

The witness told me that it looked like a 'man-bat' and was at least six feet tall. It had human-like arms and legs, though very slender. The body and head were slender, but proportionate. The wing span was approximately twelve feet and leather-like. The body was very dark in color. The face of the being was quite interesting. The witness states that it had a short, canine-like snout; similar to that of a French Bulldog. But the overall face structure resembled that of a Gothic gargoyle. The eyes did not glow or show color. He doesn't know if the being reacted to his presence.

When the being unfurled its wings and ascended, the witness could hear the loud flapping of the wings, even though his windows were closed. The witness stated that the overall shape of the winged being reminded him of the 'Man-Bat' character in Batman, though it was more slender and less intimating.

The witness had not heard of the previous sightings. He later contacted a friend, who told him about the rash of sightings in the Chicago area and where to report his encounter. The witness had no physical reaction to this sighting, but was initially shocked and confused by what he was looking at.

This report included the best facial description received by us, even though I believe that there are several winged beings with varied descriptions.

THE NEXT DAY, I received an email from a witness who provided an intense encounter account:

"Hello, I just found your email and want to tell you what I saw. Please do not contact me. I live near the elementary school on Central Park Ave. Last night, Tuesday, September 26, 2017, at 9:15PM I heard the neighbor dog barking like crazy. I looked out the back door and turned on the porch light. We saw this monster bat spread open its wings in my back yard. My son saw it too. It took off into the air in just a second or two. We both fell to our knees. I am so scared by this. My son drew this sketch. The red eyes were very bright and it looked at us."

The sketch was very dramatic, but I was confused somewhat by the report. It took me awhile to figure out that this sighting was in Little Village, and very close to the previous sightings. I believe the school, that the witness is referring to, is the Castellanos Elementary School located at 2524 S. Central Park Avenue. I made an attempt to reach out to the witness and see if they would reconsider adding more information or possibly talk to me.

I soon received an email that included a telephone number for me to contact. I was able to talk to the witness the next evening:

The woman and her adult son witnessed the winged being and are sticking to most of the original story; though there were a few revisions. I asked how long they observed the being, and I was told by the son that he watched it for at least 10 seconds. His mother had an immediate reaction to it and dropped to the floor.

He continued to watch the being until it flapped its wings and ascended quickly. He said that the wings were about fifteen feet wide when fully open, judging by the width of the yard. He thought the height was about six to seven feet. He never heard a sound, even when it flapped the wings. It was standing in front of the garage at the end of the yard, so there was a good backdrop for him to see detail. The son actually wrote the original email; seems his mother doesn't use a computer.

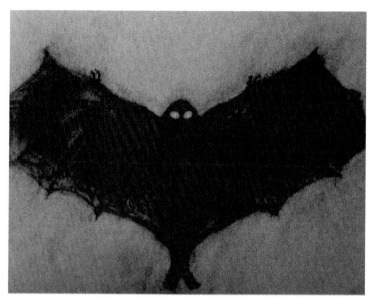

Witness' rendering of the backyard sighting in Little Village.

I asked if he would talk to an investigator. He said possibly, but they would not be able to meet at his mother's house. He also told me that his girlfriend drew the sketch this morning from his description. He also said that the drawing was very close to what he witnessed.

He told me that he was hesitant to make a report, but his girlfriend and her brother had heard of the sightings and gave him my information. We had a pleasant conversation; but he is concerned for his mother. She is not reacting well to the sighting.

The conversation with the witness cleared up a lot of my confusion. I asked the witness if he would mind talking to Manuel in person, but he was unsure if that could be arranged. His concern for his elderly mother is a big factor in his reluctance, which can surely be understood.

At this point, we had received four reports within a six block radius in the Little Village neighborhood. The Task Force was beginning to formulate a 'working' theory as to why some of these entities may be manifesting in such close proximity. At least with this group of incidents, we may hopefully have been given an opportunity to explain the influx of these entities with a greater position of certainty.

A GREATER PRESENCE by the Task Force in the neighborhood was now warranted. Since Manuel was fluent in Spanish and was cognizant of the culture within Little Village, he took the lead on this part of the investigation. He and his son began to post flyers throughout the area of the sightings, and began to setup trail cameras in strategic locations. As well, he conducted interviews with some of the business owners and residents. In short order, Manuel's persistence began to pay off. UFO Clearinghouse received an account on Sunday, October 1, 2017: Date: September 24, 2017. Time: About 8:45PM. Location: 2600 block of South Drake Avenue. Witnesses: Three (mother and two adult children):

"We were walking home from Sunday evening mass and were walking our usual route up Drake Avenue toward our house.

As we walked we noticed what looked like a very tall man dressed in black standing out in the middle of the road underneath a street light. We didn't pay it much attention as we assumed that it was just a regular person in the road and wearing black clothing.

The man then stretched his arms up above his head and suddenly a pair of very large wings spread out from behind him, which must have been over 10 feet wide and were solid black. Even though this man was standing under a street light, there was not a lot of detail to this man.

As we walked closer, we noticed that the man turned and walked, more like hopped toward the sidewalk ahead of us. It was then that it turned toward us and we saw that it had a pair of glowing red eyes. My mother uttered the words "Madre de Dios" and crossed herself and then said to us that it looked like a Duende, which is the Spanish word for 'a Goblin.' We stopped and I stood in front of my mom trying to shield her. The man then made a loud screech and then it opened its wings and shot up in the air. You could hear the sound of wings flapping as it rose up in the air and passed over us and out of sight as it continued flying down the street and out of sight. My mother was visibly shaking and was praying, when I turned back to her. We reassured her that it was over and the thing was gone. I asked my brother to help assist her during the rest of the way home.

When we got home, my brother said that my mother told him that she could feel a strong sense of evil coming from this thing. She was certain that this thing was sent to do harm to someone and that she felt sorry for whoever it was sent after. I am certain that whatever it was that we saw, it was not a bird but something from outside of this world."

The description 'goblin' was unique, and I never remember

that term being used to describe any of the flying beings we were investigating.

Manuel soon contacted the witnesses and later added the following information:

> I talked to the eldest brother, (the person who made the original report) and he stated that he had heard from others about the sightings and that he could report it to UFOCH from a flyer posted at a local grocery store. I spoke on two occasions with him and then once to the younger brother regarding their sighting. The third witness was unwilling to speak with me in regard to her sighting but did provide details via her eldest son. Both siblings were able to recall their sightings in detail and both gave similar descriptions when interviewed separately. Neither of the witnesses embellished upon their sighting and neither witness contradicted the others testimony. When I asked if either one would accompany me back to the spot of the sighting, I was told that they would accompany me, but would only do it during the daylight hours and would absolutely not do it after dark. It was apparent that both witnesses were quite shaken and that they believe that what they saw was real.

This was the fifth confirmed sighting within a seven block radius in the Little Village neighborhood and it is the investigator's opinion that this sighting is valid and that the witnesses are credible. This sighting warrants further investigation. The proximity of the sighting to other reported sightings also warrants further investigation and a follow-up with all witnesses.

MANUEL RECEIVED another report via a flyer a few days later:

"I was coming out of Dulcelandia (3253 W. 26th St. in Little Village) on Wednesday, October 4, 2017, with my husband and we looked up and saw what looked like a large black bat fly over us. It flew across the street and over some trees. From what we saw, it must have been at least six feet tall and had wings that must have been ten feet in width. It looked like it had bat wings as they looked like they were part of its arms. As it flew over it was making a very loud screaming sound and was flapping its wings as it flew over the trees. I tried to get a picture of it, but it was over the trees in seconds and gone. We walked down the block to see if maybe we could see it before turning around and heading back to our car.

We I saw a flyer at a restaurant that we visited the next day and took down the information, and submitted this report. You can reach us at (number omitted for privacy reasons) and ask for (name omitted for privacy reasons). We are willing to talk about what we saw."

This sixth sighting report expanded the Little Village location group to a twelve block radius. Manuel spent the following weekend on-site, gathering as much information as possible.

The Task Force, now more than ever, strongly believed that the incidents in the neighborhood had an occult-based genesis from somewhere within the local populace. Tobias Wayland, Rosemary Ellen Guiley and I had each had some experience and personal awareness when it came to magic and conjuring. This rationale may not explain why there have been numerous sightings of a similar winged being throughout the Chicago metro region, but we were upbeat and undaunted nonetheless. We were seeking a panacea that would connect all the pieces.

17

'JEEPERS CREEPERS'

I HAVE INVESTIGATED FLYING humanoid sightings since 1981, when I first included cryptid creatures as a part of my paranormal research after a personal unexplained encounter.

Since the beginning of the millennium, a specific term has surfaced as part of the description of several of the sightings; 'Jeepers Creepers.' If you are familiar with modern horror films, then you'll have an idea of what I'm talking about.

In 2001, an American-German horror film, that took its name from the 1938 song 'Jeepers Creepers,' was released. It was a tale about two older siblings who become the targets of a demonic creature, known as the 'Creeper,' in rural Florida.

This 'Creeper' was an ancient, mysterious demon, who viciously fed on the flesh and bones of multiple human beings for 23 days every 23rd spring. The Creeper appears as a somewhat masculine, humanoid being, and usually wears a tattered, 19th century duster, wide-brimmed stetson, and tattered trousers to pass for human. His feet end in bird-like talons and his fingers have small hooks. The skin is covered in thick, dark-green scales.

His face has prominent jowls, framing a set of needle-like

teeth. The majority of his head is bald, and he has a third nostril that sits upon his nose. The Creeper is able to expand a wide fringe of webbed, insect-like appendages as a threat display. There is also a set of bat-like wings that lie folded against his back, hiding under his duster, but capable of propelling him through the air with immense force.

By any definition, the Creeper is a gruesome creature. The fact that several witnesses have compared the winged being that they encountered as resembling the Creeper is beyond my realization. I suppose it a cultural phenomenon; basically because there are few other creatures, natural or fictional, to compare to.

A few of the Chicago Phantom witnesses mentioned the Creeper character when giving a general description, though the eventual comparison came down to the bat-like wing structure and the ability to instantly launch itself into flight.

During the same time period that we were receiving reports in the Chicago area, we were also receiving accounts of similar winged beings in other locations throughout the United States and Canada.

Most of the sightings were very brief and without much detail, but a few specific reports compounded our curiosity. In particular, there was one account where the witnesses used the Creeper comparison as well as other factors that sounded very familiar:

"It was about 4:00AM early this morning, October 2, 2017. All the dogs started barking in the neighborhood. I have a big pit bull that was barking and he tried busting my fence down to go towards something. I stepped outside and heard something on neighbor's roof scratching. So I let my dog loose. I've never seen him so mad.

I went towards my neighbor's house from my porch and saw a man standing on her roof. But when my dog started trying to jump the gate, this man flew straight up with bat-like wings. It kind of reminded me of 'Jeepers Creepers' character. I don't know what I saw, but it was creepy. I'm in Ballinger, TX. - JF."

The witness, JF asked me to call him. He found my email on the internet while searching for any information on this flying being.

The witness stated that he lives in Ballinger, Texas which is approximately sixty miles south of Abilene, TX. When he went outside to check on why the dogs were barking, he took a shotgun with him. He noticed this humanoid standing on the neighbor's roof, which he said was five to six feet tall, dark in color with a thin body and had human-like arms and legs. It was looking up into the sky. There was enough light coming from his porch for him to be able to get a good look.

When his pit bull tried to jump the neighbor's fence, the being looked down at his dog and its large eyes lit up bright reddish-yellow; so much so, that it obscured the face. Then suddenly, a pair of wing sprung out from its back, which extended approximately thirteen to fifteen. JF described the wings as those of a giant bat. It then flapped its wings once, and quickly shot straight up into the sky.

When I talked to JF, it was obvious that he had no idea what he had witnessed and was quite shook up. He was surprised to come across the reports from Chicago and wanted to ask if the being he witnessed may have been related to those sightings.

It had become apparent that sightings of winged humanoids were beginning to surface in locations other than Chicago and the surrounding area. I wanted to continue focusing on the Chicago incidents, but I didn't want to ignore the rising number of accounts from other locations that had been reported to the Task Force. If a photograph or other pertinent evidence devel-

oped from these other sightings, this would be a positive compo-
nent to our overall understanding of these winged beings.

IN EARLY JUNE 2017, I received an account from the
Bronx, NY:

*"A few years back, 2011 or so, I was living in the Bronx. My
Mum and I were outside having yarns and laughs. Suddenly
she said that she heard this strange noise, what sounded like an
aircraft or flying object cutting through the air. At first I
thought she was joking, until I heard it myself. She pointed to
the sky and said; "look baby, it looks like a bat." I was like;
"that's too big to be a bat." Then she was like; "well it must be
a weather balloon."*

*She then walks back in the house strangely, so I sat
waiting for her to back come out. She came back with coffee,
when I heard something cutting through the tree tops.
Whatever it was had landed in my neighbor's tree (it had been
cut back a lot, but had enough leaves covering it). It had a big
thump to it when it landed. Mum ran inside when she heard it.
I was freaking out, but couldn't help but stare.*

*As I walked to the fence, I noticed that there was no wind
whatsoever. As I was trying to get a better look, a big deep
breath blew into my face. I was startled, stood back and said;
"if you're a man of God show your face now! But if not, just
leave please." As I was stepping back I saw it. Shocked like a
stunned mullet, this big wind roared up and with a huge
thump, it flew into mid-air.*

*Damn, that thing looked like Jeepers Creepers. Big tall
dark man; big built solid body, seven to eight foot and it looked
like it had wings like a bat! Shocked, I ran into the house and*

went directly to my room, laid down thinking about what I witnessed.

The next morning, Mum left to go to work, so I decided to rake the backyard. Then my neighbor yelled; "Hey Sis, what happened to you last night?" He then said; "you're lucky it didn't take you!" He yarned about an old folk tale; that there was a man with wings like a bat that used to come around every now and then; take women back to where he lived and makes them his wives. The way he described it, matching what I'd seen. Still to this day I don't know for sure what or who this thing was?"

I believe that the witness may have lived in an Arawak (Curaçao, Netherlands Antilles) immigrant neighborhood in the Bronx. I'm not familiar with the folklore, but I have heard similar accounts from other Caribbean nationals.

GOING BACK A FEW YEARS, in July 2015, I recall a report I received from Cherry Hill, NJ:

"I came across your site looking for answers to something my daughter and I had seen in the sky. There are similar sightings by other people in the area. I am from Cherry Hill, NJ, and approximately two years ago to this day, my daughter and I were riding our bikes. It was bright that night due to a full moon. Not many clouds in the sky, but a few that would occasionally darken the moonlight.

We stopped by a friend's house. Her and her two daughters came out and we were all just talking. I happened to look up in the sky and there's this flying, long human-shaped thing with a wing span seven to eight feet wide. It reminded me of the movie 'Jeepers Creepers.' My mouth just kind of opened and I was speechless, pointing as it went behind the cloud near the moon. I told them what I had just witnessed. Everyone kind of giggled and I told them it did not come out of the cloud yet and to continue looking.

Well, to our eyes it appeared again. My daughter just stood there watching it, repeating herself; "Mom what is that?" I know she had that same hard-to-swallow feeling I did, while my friend's two girls ran inside screaming. We watched as it flapped and soared near the moon till it disappeared into the clouds again and never came out.

I know what I saw that night, but wouldn't know what to call it except a flying human-like creature. It's an experience I would never take back and when I hear others, I really want to believe they had seen the same thing. My daughter to this day feels there is so much out there we really don't know much about. What is myth and what is real?"

An interesting aspect to this account is that there had been a series of unexplained sightings throughout central New Jersey during the same time period. Those witnesses were describing flying beings that resembled 'dragons;' huge winged creatures that defied conventional zoology. I had received three different accounts, all stating that these 'dragons' looked like the flying beasts from mythology.

IN JANUARY 2017, I was made aware of another encounter that took place in the mid-1980s in Oregon:

"I experienced something in the mid-1980s. I did not know what it was until twenty years later when I saw the movie

'Jeepers Creepers.' That's the only way can explain the creature I saw.

I was driving from work, using a country road. I worked evenings and late nights. I saw an object above the ground, flying over the roadway and coming towards me. I thought it may have been an owl and that I'd better slow down. Then it appeared and it looked like the 'Creeper' creature. Then it disappeared and I thought that I must have imagined it.

Then all of a sudden, underneath my car there was like a thump, thump, thump. I thought I'd driven over something. I looked back. I looked to the right and to the left, in my mirrors; you know, the sides, turned my head. All of a sudden, I see these arms, a hand and a wing; then the face. The eyes were an orange color, but human-like and very large. The nose; it looked human. But the skin; you could see the veins on the wings, leather-like. It was like if you held your ear up to a light, you could kind of see right through it a little bit.

It then crawled onto the top of the car and moved over in front of the windshield; with its arms and wings flapping here and there. The next thing I know I heard another thump, thump, thump. It was now on its backside, on the ground and I'm still moving. I was wondering if it was still alive. I don't want to hit and run anything, even though I was very scared. I slowed down for some unknown reason and watched it.

It then slowly began to stand up on its human-like legs. It then turned and looked right at me. It appeared like it was crippled, struggling to stretch its wings. I continued to watch. After a while, it seemed that it was fine. It turned towards the field that had a wood railing, with an adjoining group of trees and moon in the background. It flew but it hit the ground again because it was wobbling. But it got up and it flew again. Then it disappeared into the trees.

To this day I'm still kind of shaken about it. I never knew

what I had seen. Then just two months ago I looked it up on the internet; about the movie, about the creature and it still doesn't make sense. Did other people see this thing before and then make the movie? This was in Oregon outside of Amity. I lived way up in Molalla and I traveled through a lot of counties to get to my job. After that encounter, it took me several weeks before I drove on that road again."

IN SEPTEMBER 2012, my friend and colleague cryptid investigator JC Johnson relayed to me information that involved an unknown flying being that had been terrorizing a family on the Dine Navajo native lands near the Four Corners area of New Mexico. I later wrote a report that I posted on my blog:

JC Johnson and his team were contacted on Friday 9/21/2012, in reference to a series of disturbing incidents occurring at a residence in the Four Corners area of New Mexico. The family had experienced loud clawing sounds and indiscernible growls coming from outside their home. The daughter has also endured clawing outside her bedroom window, as well as unexplained activity within the home. She woke to claw marks on her back and has noticed items moved in her bedroom. There have been several attempts to confront this being but in each instance it has eluded the efforts.

There has been damage to the house and a vehicle as a result of these attacks. Deep claw and chew marks can be seen on the truck headlight housing and grill. There have been a few three-claw prints left on the side of the house and on the ground around the residence.

I talked to JC through Skype soon after receiving the video. He added a few interesting details.

There were two separate descriptions presented to JC. One depiction was that this being resembled the 'Creeper' from the 'Jeepers Creepers' horror film series. A more detailed summary was offered by a witness who observed this being while it was sitting on the ground. It was covered in gray hair and that a three-clawed appendage was visible. The torso to head height of this being was about five feet sitting, which would make it approximately eight to nine feet in full height. There is an indication that the being has wings which would explain the odd patches of trampled corn stalks in the field as it would fly and then land indiscriminately.

There seems to be a supernatural aspect to this being. The experiences of the daughter and the claw marks on her body must be taken into consideration. At this point, it's impossible to distinguish its intent.

The activity continued for a few weeks longer, until the daughter decided to leave the home and live at another location several hours away. It seems that her presence somehow precipitated the activity. I believe that this being may have been a 'thought-form' entity that was unconsciously created by the daughter; seemingly because she had wanted to leave the reservation and strike out on her own.

This theory, if true, may also have some validity in relation to the Chicago sightings; especially in the Little Village neighborhood. Is it possible that one person, or even a collective group of people, are manifesting a winged being? This is just a singular premise that the Task Force is contemplating.

Allow me to explain the 'thought-form' hypothesis, in relation to the creation and manifestation of a cryptid being.

A few years ago, two Wisconsin teenage girls were accused of luring their friend into the woods and stabbing her nineteen times, to prove their loyalty to a fictional character made popular by an online urban legends forum. This entity is referred to as the 'Slender Man.'

Dressed in a black suit and with no visible face, the Slender Man is an apparition with arms that stretch wide to entrap his chosen prey. Towering high, the Slender Man hunts children with a voracious appetite, stalking them through parks and play grounds, and has even been known to attack children within their dreams. Due to his attire the Slender Man has been linked to the notorious 'Men in Black,' who are thought to be Government agents who harass and threaten UFO witnesses, and who some believe to be aliens themselves. The only problem is that the Slender Man is a fictional character.

The Slender Man was born within the 'Something Awful' forums in 2009, when a thread was created to challenge members to create fake photo-shopped paranormal photographs. The idea however was not just to create these images, but to also filter them through the internet, in a bid to convince those who sought out such things, that the images created were authentic 'real' ghost/alien photographs.

Despite the Slender Man being a complete fabrication, this legend spread like wild-fire throughout the internet as a successful 'internet meme', a phrase used to describe a catch-phrase or concept that spreads quickly from person to person via the internet, much like an esoteric inside joke that evolves with time.

A YouTube sensation of sorts the 'Marble Hornets Project' was a series of video clips that were supposedly recorded by a teenager named 'Alex.' The segments of video taken from Alex's camcorder tapes follow him as he becomes increasingly concerned by the fact that, 'something' sinister, is apparently stalking him.

While Alex himself has mysteriously vanished, the video

clips he left behind him become increasingly disturbing, as the Slender

Man peers from distant corners. The 'Marble Hornets Project' had greatly increased the range of the Slender Man myths reach, with some unfamiliar with the legends origin taking it at face-value, and they in turn spread the legends grip further still.

Like the Tulpa of Tibetan Buddhism and mysticism, thought-forms are brought into existence merely through power of will and strength of mind. A Tulpa is defined as 'a humanoid thought-form' and likened to a personal 'genie' that you create using thought energy. Once created, the Tulpa can be put to practical use to help you in all sorts of ways.

But, is it possible that if enough people believe in something, that this belief alone could give birth to its form?

In John Keel's 1975 authored book; 'The Mothman Prophecies,' he deals with Tulpas early in his narrative and, now and then, throughout the text. It is also interesting to note, that the native people indigenous to the Point Pleasant, WV area, along with other tribes throughout the continent, had for centuries recorded similar phenomena as a part of their lore.

In the past, there had been well-coordinated research trials that focused on the manifestation of entities. The groups included people who were known to have particular abilities in ESP, psychic, channeling, or other physical or mental specialties. These trials were dubbed 'The Philip Experiment' and 'The Skippy Experiment.'

The experiments were repeated several times with different groups, who eventually created several entity manifestations that were able to communicate with raps and taps. At the beginning, the stated goal was to eventually create an apparition. Towards the end of the experiment, and after several years of operation, some in the group felt that they were close to reaching that goal. But unfortunately, interest in the experiment waned and activities were discontinued.

As the result of these experiments, some people may conclude that this proves that ethereal entities and cryptids don't exist, that such things are in our minds only. Others may say that our unconscious could be responsible for this kind of phenomena some of the time. Regardless there is no way to prove that certain unknown entities don't exist. The manifestations in the experiment were simply psychokinetic anomalies manufactured by the collective human conscious. The only certain conclusion is that there is much to our existence and beyond that is still unexplained.

I personally believe in some of these tenets associated with

thought forms, but defined a bit differently. True mediumship, in my opinion, is an instilled gift. I don't think that it can be learned or taught. I do believe that spirits are remnant energy that has the qualification and intelligence to communicate as well as pass through portals (worm holes) between this world and other locations throughout the universe. I feel that the afterlife is like a 'way station,' where these life energies remain after they leave their earthbound environment. Some of these former earthbound energies evolve into 'helpers' for living beings, while others are integrated and merged with other living spirits. There is nothing religious or dogmatic with my theories, it's just what I have hypothesized after being subjected to the supernatural.

In the case of the Chicago flying humanoids and other related phenomena, if thought-form manifestation is a credible concept, we will need to find the genesis of creation and the means used for transforming this entity into a palpable being.

I RECEIVED another brief sighting report on Sunday, October 8, 2017:

"I was writing to share my sighting of the Chicago Mothman. I was walking towards the Chicago Ave. Redline entrance from work when I made the sighting. It happened to be around 10:15/10:20PM CT on Saturday, October 7. I happened to look up to my left, when I saw an object drifting in the sky. Upon a closer look, I was able to see the object was dark grey in color and seemed to have a large wing span. It started to drift up, but then dived down. It ducked between buildings but then reappeared on the other side. I was standing on Chicago Ave. and Wabash Ave (witness was looking south along Wabash Ave).

After the object reappeared, it passed between a few more buildings but then flew towards the lake. - J S."

I contacted the witness for follow-up information:

"From my distance it was a little hard to make out details of the object. It kept moving rather quickly and very fluid-like. The wings were about equal length if not a bit longer than the object itself. They also flapped a few times, but seemed to have glided more than flapped. I could tell the object was quite large. I easily ruled out it being a bird. - JS."

The winged being must have had significant size in order for the witness to make it out, especially at night; though I assume the area is well-lit. The witness' location was only two blocks south of the Sofitel Chicago Magnificent Mile Hotel on 20 E Chestnut St. This is where the gray humanoid was seen on the building roof.

After receiving this account, I sensed that there was a good possibility that the sightings and reports may begin to wane. The cold weather would soon begin in the upper Midwest. But to this point, there hasn't been any evidence to suggest that these winged beings couldn't withstand the cold temperatures. Some of the Mothman sightings in the

Point Pleasant area were during the winter, though I'm not suggesting that the Chicago sightings are related in any way to the Mothman.

A POST ON THE MIDLOTHIAN, Illinois 'Topix' forum caught my attention on October 23, 2017. The sighting occurred on the evening of Thursday, October 19, 2017:

> "I was on my way delivering a pizza in Midlothian on Thursday night, October 19, 2017, and was at the dead end on Waverly Ave. and Clifton Park Ave. Went to turn my truck and saw a HUGE dark figure standing on a concrete ledge in front of a massive wood fence. It was BIGGER than that fence!!! LIKE TEN FEET TALL!!
>
> This thing was swaying in the wind. I turned my brights on it and this thing was like a DEMON... NOT A MAN, that had a dark color like a dirty grey skin. It opened its wings and flew off in a second, sideways right above the houses. I did make a call and they said it would be looked into. WTF? – Alex."

Midlothian is a southern suburb of Chicago. The concrete ledge at the end of the road was below a high wooden fence that ran along the Tri-State Tollway. If the being was as tall as the fence, then it would have easily been in the ten foot height range. I made an inquiry on the forum for further information.

The witness stated that he made a call. I assume he reported the sighting to the police.

It was around this period (mid to late October, 2017) I received several spurious reports. Some of the accounts included photographic images that seemed to have been manipulated. Up until this time, we had only a handful of suspicious sighting reports.

As well, the media started to show a bit more interest in the sightings, in particular 'The Chicago Reader,' 'Vice.com,' and a few other online news sources. An up-and-coming Chicago rapper, Rich Jones, versed a song about the 'Chicago Mothman.' A music video was also produced by the 'Gnar Team' on YouTube, titled 'Mothman in Chicago.'

I believe the consensus in the Task Force was that increased press coverage may likely result in false claims. The Halloween season was in full gear, and I was hoping that this wouldn't result in an array of fictitious reports.

Things had been fairly quiet for several weeks, until Manuel received a disturbing account that had the potential of changing the dynamic of the winged humanoid sightings.

18

ATTACK!

MANUEL MENTIONED that he had received a report of an aggressive encounter by a large winged being with arms and claws in the parking lot of Piotrowski Park in Little Village:

> *"We were parked in the parking lot of the community center in Piotrowski Park, in Chicago (the park lies within the Little Village neighborhood) at about 10:30PM. We had just both gotten off work at 10:00PM and decided to meet up at the park and spend some time together before going home. We were in my boyfriend's car talking and listening to music when it felt like something hit his car from behind. There was no one else in the parking lot except his car and mine but it felt like a car had hit him.*
>
> *My boyfriend stopped what he was doing and was going to step out to see what hit his car when something large dropped onto the hood of his car. We looked, and both screamed at the same time as we saw a pair of bright orange eyes peering back at us through the windshield. The thing that landed was solid black and was about the size of a man and had what looked*

like wings that were spread out wide. It looked right at us and then appeared to swipe the windshield with its hand. The fingers were long; much longer than a normal person and ended in what looked like claws.

It looked like it was trying to get into the car and at us, we were both screaming as it swiped the windshield three to four times. My boyfriend then grabbed a flashlight that he had in the car and shined it through the windshield at this thing. It then shrieked out loud; it sounded like what the screams of multiple people in a small room would sound like. Then it flexed its wings and took off straight up and was gone from our sight. We heard it shriek out at least twice about 1 minute apart as it probably circled the area after which we heard silence. We were both scared beyond belief and I was hysterical and crying, afraid to get out as I thought it might swoop down and attack me if I did.

We spend fifteen minutes in my boyfriend's car and eventually calmed down enough to attempt to get out of the car and sprint to my car. My boyfriend got out and escorted me to my car. Once I was inside and the doors locked, he sprinted back to his car and also got ready to leave. I have never been so scared in my entire life and when I got home, I had to go into the bathroom and compose myself before facing my family. We talked about the incident at work on Monday and that is when I decided to come home and look up information if anyone else had seen this thing. I was shocked to see so many sightings had occurred and decided to report mine.

I am willing to talk to someone about this incident, but my boyfriend is refusing to, as this would jeopardize both our jobs and our families. I am willing to talk and show you the place where it happened, but only if my name or address is not used and we can be discreet about this."

This was the eighth sighting reported from the Little Village neighborhood. This was also the most aggressive encounter reported by any of the witnesses in relation to the 2017 sightings. Manuel did interview the female witness, and would follow up by going to the location and meeting with the witness the next weekend.

This incident shed a new light on our investigation. We had previously discussed the prospect of a witness being attacked and possibly injured by one of this winged humanoids. But after this particular event, it became apparent that an injured witness could easily result in medical treatment and a report taken by police. We feared that if this scenario occurred, there may be a vigilante-type reaction by the public. How would that backlash affect the investigation?

This singular humanoid was described as possessing hands with long fingers that resembled claws. This seems to indicate that it also had arms with full motion that were detached from the wings. If this is the case, then I believe that this information may suggest, and prove, that there are definitely multiple humanoids being seen. To this point, the descriptions detailed variations in the wing and arm structures.

The specifications for the wings, up to this point, have been chronicled as Mothman-like, owl-like (Lechuza) or bat/gargoyle shaped. The Piotrowski Park witness did not mention the wing shape, but concentrated more on the swiping hand. For the most part, the beings with bat-shaped wings either had no arms or had an arm-like structure attached to the wings. It's interesting to note that the Mothman of Point Pleasant descriptions and drawings depicted the being with and without arms. Was this a matter of differing observation and recollection, or was there more than one Mothman?

Once again, we have to ask; "is there a reason why these

flying humanoids are in Chicago?" As well; "are they seeking specific people?' We have attempted to find a possible connection with the witnesses, but there really does not seem to be any.

THEN IN MID-NOVEMBER 2017, I received an interesting telephone call from a native Chicagoan who insisted that her and her family have been 'followed' by a winged Goblin-like being for forty-five years. The witness included a list of eighteen locations throughout the United States where she has either seen or encountered this winged being. She told me:

"It's a shape shifter; but I think its original form is a seven foot tall creature with wings that span six feet or so. It has a goblin-like face and ears with bat-like wings, but way more flexible. It's dark brown, almost black in color. It has red eyes that almost glow in the dark. It has claw-like feet and very long fingers and arms. Arms are not connected to the wings: they are separate. Wings are on its back, like that of a bird. It has a long tail and pointed at the end. It's extremely fast in this form. Other forms it transforms into are:

- A moth-like creature. In this form its hands and wings are attached and it's closer to six feet tall with long teeth.

- It also takes the form of a bat but bigger; three feet in size with red eyes and black in color with long teeth. It's not super-fast in this form but faster than a human being.

- It can also take on a goblin-like form, in which hands and wings are separate. It's gray and black in color with long teeth, human-like hands with long claws and sharp talons on its feet. It also drools. There are red and brown eyes, and it's approximately three and a half feet tall. It's still as fast as a cat *when it needs to move. It licks itself in this form, like it's cleaning its claws. There is also a tail maybe two feet long.*

It has been inside several homes we have lived in. It hates dogs. It perches up high to avoid being seen. It hides in the shadows, like it's stalking you: similar to a feline. It has an odor almost like a musty or moss-like scent. Once you smell it you never forget it. It's mean in nature and likes to show it's in control. No matter the form, it also has a loud screeching sound. It's hard to explain. No; I do not have a photo of it and I cannot explain why my family has seen it so many times. I have no answers but I know it's real.

―――

HERE IS AN EXAMPLE OF AN INCIDENT, which occurred on the Lake Michigan shoreline in north Indiana.

I was about 10yrs old (around 1977). We had gone to visit my cousins and went fishing. We cleaned the fish at the lake and left the fish heads and scales on the river bank. This being flew down and devoured the remains. My cousin said as long as you give back it won't bother you. They had seen it several times before."

When the witness and I talked, she described that the winged being lived in a vacant warehouse next door to their home on 1751 W. Berwyn St. in Chicago (Anderson neighborhood). This occurred during 1970-1974, and that the being was observed many times by the family. When the family moved to another residence, it continued to follow them near their new location. The being made itself known to the witness after she became an adult. No one has been able to obtain a photograph.

The witness and her family wished to remain anonymous; though the witness has been very forthcoming to me during our conversation and subsequent follow-up emails. It's obvious to me that she hoped that the encounters would eventually end.

I STARTED to look back at other winged anomaly incidents in order to gain a better sense of the Chicago sightings. There are a few select accounts where the manifestation of the flying being implied that there may have been a purpose for its presence.

I had mentioned earlier that the Drennings had visited the old West Virginia Ordinance Works for the purpose of collecting EVP evidence. They had an encounter with an unseen entity that has haunted them ever since. Later on, JD (the husband) had an incident involving an unknown winged being:

> *"My daughter (whom was three years old at the time) and I were heading home after an evening of visiting family in Davis, WV. The ride home entailed that we travel through a desolate stretch of US 219 (Seneca Trail) just north of the nearby town of Thomas, WV. I was traveling along this route just as I had hundreds of times prior, listening to my daughter sing along with the radio, when directly in front of us (at a distance of roughly sixty to seventy yards) and in line with the tree tops I noticed movement. I had to slow my vehicle slightly and allow my eyes to adjust on the object, as it was barely illuminated by the upper arc of my vehicle's high-beams.*
>
> *Upon doing this I could tell that it was flying directly towards us at a brisk pace. In a matter of only a few seconds it had closed the distance between ourselves and it to thirty to*

forty yards, and the first thing I could clearly see was the unmistakable fluttering of the being's giant wings. It flapped them a few times in order to halt its movement, then landed directly in front of us (I would estimate that it was only 20 yards away at this point), as if it was intent on impeding our progress.

At this point I was in shock at what was standing before us. The being was seven to eight feet tall (head to toe), with its folded wings towering another two to three feet above its head. It was humanoid, with a stature that I can only liken to that of a bodybuilder, and void of any hair on its head. The skin was an ashen gray, and covering it (head, torso, arms) was a tribal-like tattoo that was black in color. Its eyes were completely black. At this point my daughter has taken notice of it and is completely hysterical. I had what seemed to be a million thoughts rushing through my mind, ranging from attempting to process what I am witnessing to trying to calm my daughter and plan how we can immediately vacate the area. All the while this being is silently standing in front of our vehicle, just staring at us. This encompassed what felt like an eternity but in reality was merely ten to fifteen-seconds.

Suddenly the being opened its mouth, and emitted a high frequency shriek/scream. Upon screaming it also extended its wings from behind its back, which I noticed to be covered in black/leathery skin (much like the wings of a bat) and tattered along the lower edges. It then flapped them a few times, propelling itself aloft to a height of a few feet, then immediately flapped them in quick succession and disappeared upward and over our vehicle. I immediately accelerated my vehicle and left the area behind us as quickly as possible. Fortunately we encountered nothing further from the being. - JD."

This encounter does not suggest that this winged being was similar to the Mothman seen in and around Point Pleasant, WV. JD and his wife contacted me very soon after the Chicago sightings were becoming public knowledge, in the hope that I could help them. After their incident at the West Virginia Ordinance Works, they were subsequently subjected to unexplained paranormal activity at home and elsewhere; including bizarre telephone calls and other strangeness. The Drenning's account seems to leap right out of the pages of John Keel's 'The Mothman Prophecies.'

IN AUGUST 2017, I received an interesting account of an event that matched much of what had been reported in Chicago:

"This took place twenty years ago in Amman, Jordan. I don't remember the exact date, but it was June 1997, around midnight. I was seventeen at the time, my sister was fourteen. She was trying to get to sleep in her bedroom, but it was a hot night, so she got up and opened the window. As she got back in her bed, something crawled through the window and stood at the foot of her bed. It was fairly dark in the room, with only dim light coming through the window.

She saw a winged creature almost as tall as the ceiling, dark black with a crest on the top of its head like a pterodactyl. She couldn't make out any facial features or tell the texture of the body other than a slight sheen on the side the light was hitting it. The most notable feature she noticed were its "blazing" red eyes, as she described them. When she locked eyes with the creature, a feeling of shock, dread and fear took over her. She wanted to scream, but no sound came out. She couldn't move or look away. She "felt" the creature tell her to not make a sound, in her mind, as if it knew she was trying to scream. This lasted for about thirty-seconds as the creature stared at her silently and motionless.

Suddenly, the creature turned towards the window and darted outside like a spear with a "whoosh" sound as it exited. We lived in a fifth story apartment with a fifty foot drop out the window. A few seconds passed and she let out the most blood curdling scream I have ever heard, which made me jump out of bed in my bedroom and make a dash towards her room. I flipped the light switch on as I burst through her bedroom door to see her sitting up in her bed white as a ghost, shaking and crying.

My parents woke up and came running to her room as well. It took about 10 minutes for her to calm down enough to speak coherently. She told us that she had a nightmare. A couple of days later, she told me what actually happened. She seemed reluctant and scared to recall the details of the other night. I didn't know what to make of it and we didn't speak of it again as I felt that would be best at the time.

Fast forward twenty years and I'm reading an article about the 'Chicago Phantom.' The more eyewitness accounts I read about, the more I thought of that night. I decided to contact my sister and tell her about what I've been reading. She seemed to get mad about me bringing this back up for her. She retold the story to me and is still terrified to this day. She is angry with me for bringing the memory back to light for her, but I convinced her that the story needs to get out there because of what everyone is seeing in Chicago. Hopefully this account helps somehow, and sheds more light on whatever this thing was, if indeed it is the same creature that's turning up in Chicago. - Al."

After reading this account, I began to wonder if it were possible that a Djinn (mischievous or malevolent shape-shifting entity) may have been involved, possibly transforming itself into a flying humanoid. Could this be occurring in Chicago? I conferred with Rosemary Ellen Guiley, who has extensively written about the Djinn phenomenon. Her assessment was that it was possible and that it should be investigated further. Rosemary has been very interested in the Chicago sightings and is also a member of the Chicago Phantom Task Force. Her research into the Mothman and other flying anomalies is well-known.

IN DECEMBER 2010, I received an email from a woman (who I will refer to as 'EW') from northern Georgia who thought she had encountered a Mothman. After many months of correspondence, the witness agreed to allow me to post the event in July 2011, but only under strict circumstances:

> *"Hello, I am hoping you can shed some light on an incident I had a few years ago. I was twenty-five at the time and was driving to my friend CW's house. It was quiet at 11:30 pm as I drove south on an old country road off of the highway here in north Georgia. Very few people pass this way because it leads to nothing but a small group of houses. I turned on the radio but nothing came on. I figured it was a blown fuse, but then I started to hear weird scratching sounds coming through the speakers. It sounded like a distant voice but I couldn't understand what it was saying.*
>
> *Suddenly, something flew in front of the car and hit the windshield with enough size and force that it totally mangled the grill and hood. I immediately stopped the car. I heard what*

sounded like wings flapping on the roof, but then something rolled down the back window onto the trunk then eventually on to the road. I thought I killed whatever it was. A woman in a truck had pulled up from behind and said she saw the thing hit the road. She said that its eyes were glaring bright red. As we looked more closely at this thing it resembled a man with large bat-like wings. The woman walked back to her truck and pulled a shotgun from the back and pointed it at this bat-like creature. It was starting to move and we backed off. It slowly stood up on two large raptor-like claws, turned and stared directly at us with those terrible bright red eyes. The woman pumped the shotgun. It slowly levitated off the ground with wings spread until it was about ten feet in the air. It then instantly, let out a deafening screech as it just disappeared with a loud 'swoosh.' The woman (who I found out later was CW's aunt) and I just looked at each other.

This thing had the body of a well-built man. It had no feathers but charcoal gray skin like that of a bat with some hair on the shoulders and around the eyes and legs. When it spread its wings, it had the span of twelve feet or more. I estimate it was about eight feet tall. It had no head however, just the eyes embedded on the shoulders that had brows. I didn't notice a mouth or nose. There is no way I was going to report this and CW's aunt totally agreed. We both drove off to CW's house. I was so shook up I stayed the night.

The next morning, I went outside to inspect the car. There was a huge crack in the windshield and the grill was mangled beyond repair. The hood also had a deep twenty-five inch dent. I started to walk back to the house when I noticed something lying in the grass beside the garage. It was CW's Golden Retriever, lying dead from massive lacerations up and down its back. I just knew that thing did it.

That was three years ago and I constantly dream of this

creature. I was told by a friend that I had encountered a Mothman. It looked more like a Batman to be honest. I decided to look up a few of the sightings by others and saw your name and blog. Many of the images on Google were very similar to what I saw. I wrote to someone else about a year ago but they never got back to me. - EW."

This is not the only time I have been told that a similar winged being attacked and killed an animal. In fact, the scenario has usually been that after a kill occurs, the carcass is left for an undetermined time before it is fed upon. This is what is happening with the sightings in Pasco County, Florida. The being has killed small white-tailed deer and other animals, sometimes leaving the carcasses in piles, to be fed on at a later time. There isn't any indication that this behavior is occurring in Chicago and, in fact, there have not been any exceptional reports of missing pets or dead animals.

ONE OF THE strangest winged humanoid reports I received was in 2011. The account detailed a dark Mothman-like humanoid in southwest Alaska. The witness (Nate) stated that he and others had encountered this being. I later caught up with the witness, who confirmed that there was another incident by a villager the previous winter; but he had few details. The following narrative is the witness' own recollection:

"My first encounter with this thing that most people call the Mothman was when I was nine years old and I remember it clearly like it was yesterday. I was walking back from my uncle's place. I was walking on the sidewalk and I saw this

man standing on top of my father's house close to the edge facing west. He was all black and looked like a man. He stood about seven or eight feet tall. I shouted out at him but he acted like he didn't hear me. I said; "Hey you; who are you?" I kept trying to get his attention; it was like I wasn't there. When I yelled, "Hey, you're standing on my house. Who are you?", he looked at me for a few seconds.

His face seemed like a normal person's face until it slowly opened its eyelids and I saw a red glow. His eyes were glowing, not a red light but a glow. I froze and just stared at him. He stood there looking at me for about ten-seconds and looked away, then jumped really high and far. I'd say he jumped about forty feet high and seventy to eight feet away and as soon as he seemed to fall down, very long and large wings came out of his back and flapped twice. In those two flaps he traveled about one hundred feet and flew right over the high school.

Since that day I never spoke to anyone about it because I thought I saw the devil. I freaked out so bad I looked out for it every day to make sure it wasn't around. That is my first encounter with that thing. Its body was like a man's and his face is like a man's too; but his eyes are what make it so scary and weird. Those wings are very long and large. His whole body was all black. Not skin but blackness was covering him; I can't explain. I'm not the only one in my village that saw this thing but after that there have been many sightings here and in other villages. Even to a point that the thing goes into people's houses while they sleep. That happened to someone I know. – Nate."

I had decided that, before I post further encounters in Nate's village, I needed to know more details about these sightings. These specific occurrences were experienced in and around the coastal village of Tununak, Alaska, located on the northeast coast of Nelson Island, about 110 miles northwest of Bethel. The population of the community consists of 96.9% Alaska Native. Tununak is a traditional Yup'ik Eskimo village, with an active fishing and subsistence lifestyle.

I received some follow-up information from Nate:

"I don't know the thing's real name, I just call it a Mothman. Most of the people here know it as the 'Black Devil,' because it comes around and suddenly very bad things start happening. Sometimes it just seems to be watching and nothing happens or very weird things happen. Some people will experience an ability of some sort for a short time and then suddenly they're back to normal. If you ask me, I think that the Mothman is not a physical being. I think it's an energy formed from somewhere or someplace that takes character when encountered by an individual. When encountered by a person with a certain belief system the Mothman takes on a form according to the person's view of reality. That's one theory of mine to explain its appearance to people. Some people will say it looked like an angel with red eyes. Some will say it looks like a cowboy standing 9 feet tall with glowing red eyes. Others will say it looked like a 6 feet tall man that can walk through walls. So to tell you my thoughts of the name of the thing I would say maybe its name is 'Leviathan' from the book of Job in the Bible. That would be the closest name I got for it. Why I had so many encounters with it? I have no idea. I do know that there have been encounters in other villages."

The following narratives are Nate's description of his subsequent experiences with this being:

"My second encounter was when I was a teenager. It was a winter night and I was riding on a snow machine with my cousin. We saw a light on the north hill. We thought it was a snow machine so we went to go and see who it was. When we got close to the hill the light disappeared. We were able to see every part of the hill. The light just vanished, so we were going to go back home. We turned the snow machine around as cousin said he had to urinate, so I waited for him to finish.

While I was waiting I saw a black object on the ground, darker than all the other things on the ground. It was getting taller like something was coming out of the ground. As soon as it reached 7 feet tall or so it started to come at us fast. I told my cousin to look at the thing. He started to freak out and ran to the snow machine, started it and looked back at it. He yelled it's getting very close so I looked back. It seemed to be one hundred feet or so away and coming fast. I screamed to my cousin to take off fast. I was so freaked out I closed my eyes. We were going at least fifty miles an hour on the snow machine.

I looked back to see how far we got from it but that thing was getting closer, I estimate at fifteen to twenty feet away from us. It was then I noticed the wings, but they were not flapping. It was like that thing was floating over the ground. I couldn't see any eyes on it; no red eyes, just all black. I was screaming to my cousin to go faster but the thing just got closer and closer like speed was nothing to it. When we reached the village the thing stopped and turned around.

My cousin just kept going fast on the town road going about sixty miles an hour until we got close to my grandmother's place. He slammed on the brakes as we jumped off of the snow machine and ran into the house. We told everyone inside about what was chasing us. My grandmother said it was the 'Black Devil' and told us to stop being 'bad kids.'

The third encounter was when I was twenty-two years old and at home playing on the Ouija board. I was talking with the board and it said it was the 'DEVIL' so I foolishly asked it to possess me. It said; 'NO.' I asked why, and it said; 'WRATH,' so I stopped asking it questions. Suddenly the room started to get cold even with the furnace running. I wrapped myself with my blanket but I was just getting colder.

I also felt the need to look through the window; like something was telling me to. I again felt this urge to look, so I got up, went over to the window and looked outside. I saw a man standing next to the steps of my neighbor's house, just looking at me. I could tell he was staring at me though I thought it was one of my neighbors. So I went outside to talk to him. I called his name but he never replied. The street light was shining on him but I was unable to see his face, like he was covered in a black cloud or some sort of blackness. I kept trying to get him it to recognize me but received no answer from him.

I took out my Zippo lighter which I had just filled with lighter fluid and hadn't used it since. I flicked it on and tried to see his face but I still couldn't see it. When I got closer my Zippo turned off as if that thing blew at it. I tried to relight it but I was unable to do so. Suddenly I heard a quiet voice saying in my head to 'back away.' So I backed off slowly, not turning my back until I got to the road.

When I reached the road I took off running as fast as I could to my place. I looked out the window to see if it was still there and it was still staring at me. I started to look for a flashlight so I could see what or who it was. When I found the flashlight I looked out the window and noticed that it was moving off to the road.

I decided to follow it. When I looked closely it didn't seem to be walking; it was floating away. Dogs would start barking *as it passed houses. I was chasing it holding a flashlight hoping I could get a look at his face. I was too slow to get close but fast enough to keep up behind it, like it was going slow to make sure I was behind it but fast enough to stay far ahead of me. It was luring me to him but I kept chasing it. When it started getting closer to the church it slowed down and circled the church, like it didn't want to get close. It continued to move on and I just continued chasing it. When we reached the end of the village I stopped.*

I felt weird, like that thing was trying to get me to go out onto the tundra in the dark. I turned around and quickly walked home.

There are other encounters with this thing that many of the people in the world know as 'Mothman.' But here, we know it as the 'Black Devil.' He has been around for very long time and has been seen by many people here. He has done a lot of things that scare villagers, like being at a location where someone dies the very next day and on the very exact spot where he was. When he comes around that means something very bad is going happen.

I don't call him the 'Black Devil.' I disagree with that term; I just call him the 'Black Man with Red Eyes' or 'Dark Man' because he's surrounded by a blackness or a black cloud.

There was an encounter where a guy was out hunting and saw it with a couple of his friends. They tried to get its attention but it never responded back. They tried shooting next to it but he never got spooked by the gunshot. There are many other encounters but these are not mine, so I can't say exactly what happened. I just hear the stories."

Nate was convinced that the 'Dark Man' was a harbinger of bad tidings and posed a danger whenever it was seen. I'm quite sure that there was a bit of superstition and local legend mixed in along the way. But there is no doubt that these winged humanoids create fear and dread wherever they turn up. Was this being, in any possible way, related to the Mothman or the winged humanoids that are involved in the Chicago sightings? I believe that, in some situations, these beings have a purpose; but can also become dangerous if provoked. Let's hope it never gets to that point in Chicago.

19

COMMUNION WITH A MOTHMAN

I HAVE QUESTIONED THE 'HARBINGER' or 'bad omen' theory associated with the Mothman and other wing humanoids. That being said, I have received several accounts that were directly related to the Silver Bridge collapse at Point Pleasant, WV. One account, in particular, is a haunting suggestion that the Mothman may have been attempting to convey a message.

I received this account from a friend ('DR') who had previously shared her paranormal experiences with me. The following remarkable narrative may very well add credence to the Mothman phenomena and, frankly, I have no reason not to believe the story. I have not edited the original text except for a few minor errors. I realize that the allegory is a bit hard to follow at certain spots, but I wanted to save the integrity of DR's thoughts and emotion:

> "In 1967, two weeks before the collapse of the Silver Bridge in Point Pleasant, WV, a phone call came to our house south of Lancaster, Ohio. It was from dad's friends in southwestern WV. Someone else in our house answered the phone because

my dad was busy watching the evening news, so he yelled to whoever answered it to ask them what they wanted. The answer was that they had some trouble over in WV and needed dad to come down. He asked what the trouble was and the person on the other end said it was a big bird. Well, we'd just seen a piece on this on the news and the anchor who reported it laughed about it. Dad laughed and said that was a good one and to tell the person this and then hang up.

A short time after the phone rang again. This was when long distance cost an arm and a leg so dad asked what was going on and again it was that they had this big bird that had done a lot of damage and they needed help to hunt it down. He took the phone call then and we all heard him saying; "All of my guns and all of my ammunition? What the heck is going on down there?" There were a couple of okays and then I heard him ask why this man's daughter needed to talk to me. It was explained to me that this youngest girl had what they thought was an imaginary friend but asking to talk with me was a good sign that she was coming out of this mentally and emotionally and I was to play along. It was supposed to be for her own good. I was nine years old and she was maybe a few months behind me. I got on the phone and she asked if this was (my name) and I said yes. I asked what her name was and she said what it was.

I'd met her once before and she was very introverted and really didn't mix with us. She showed us rocks and bugs but didn't really get involved in getting to know us. That's why I was shocked that this girl asked for me by name. I told her she had a good memory and she said it wasn't her memory that she got my name from! I thought, OK, she's a bit touched as they say, LOL.

I asked where she got my name in order to ask for me and she said it was her friend who was a man; but wasn't a man. I said, "Okay, who is this friend and what does he want with me?" She began to relate that in the course of talking one day he told her my name and said he wanted her to contact me and ask me to come down there to talk to him. I said I'd have to talk to my parents first.

I got off the phone and dad wanted to know what was up with this girl. I said there was no way she knew my name. He asked where she got it then. I told him and he got a little alarmed and called their house to ask some questions about this man that 'wasn't a man' and who he might be. They assured him that it wasn't anyone near them as they were out on a quiet country road with only a few neighbors. She said this friend of hers wasn't one of them. They'd checked the woods where she said she'd met with him and never found any footprints or signs that anyone had been there with her. So, because this was urgent we packed up quick and headed down there from central Ohio.

We waited in line to cross the Silver Bridge across from Point Pleasant. A cross member on the top of this bridge on our side of the river was swinging back and forth as it was not attached on one end. The bridge clanged and made all sorts of racket when a car was crossing it. I was told to sit back and rest my eyes because the sunlight was very bright that day and I was getting hot. I felt my eyes get heavy; like I was slipping right into a comfortable rest. The next thing I knew I heard screaming and found myself horizontal above my brothers clawing at the window screaming to be let out that the bridge was going to go into the river.

Dad got me calmed down and asked when this was going to happen. I had to rest, I was exhausted. So, I sat back and slipped asleep once again and again I found myself across my brothers with my siblings holding my legs and ankles to keep me from going out the window. I realized I was screaming *again and clawing at the window. I asked what was going on and they all said I'd been OK and then suddenly lunged for the window to claw my way out while screaming hard. Mom said to beat me for it and so did my siblings. Dad on the other hand told them to hush while he walked me through what I was seeing when I woke up doing this.*

I was in a vehicle and it was falling off that bridge into the river below and I saw every inch of the fall to the water and below the water even. I was horrified when it was slow enough for me to see all of this clearly. Dad asked if we'd get across OK that day and when we were supposed to go back home. I searched my mind and saw it was OK to cross. He had me tell him what would cause the bridge to fall and then show it to him on the other side once we got there. When he saw what I'd seen in my mind on the Ohio side before we got to the WV side he was utterly horrified.

Structurally that bridge should not have been in use at all. I won't go into that part but to say that I got it absolutely right on each and every count. He was quiet all the way there except occasionally he would ask me when this would happen. I remember looking in my mind and telling him it would happen in about two weeks.

Two weeks to the day we were sitting watching the TV when a news alert came across to say it had fallen into the river. Mom got a calendar right away and checked it to make sure how long it had been. She cried a bit and then asked me to come over to her. She thanked me for saving all their lives. I'd forgotten all about what happened two weeks prior because it was traumatic not just for my visions but for what happened at the people's house!

I hope this helps others, Lon, but I can't have identifying information come back to me about this for certain reasons. I will continue. We drove a long time before arriving and dad went in to talk to these people as we set up our tent to sleep outside. The man came out and said to put it away because we wouldn't want to be sleeping out there with the troubles they had down there. It didn't make sense to any of us how a big bird could be scaring these people that bad but they were scared badly. While the adults got the low down we kids went up into the woods to take care of the imaginary friend thing.

The older kids checked everything out to make sure there was no one and nothing to harm us when they left. We were not far into the woods and it was not all that thick with growth. The driveway was pretty wide and it was a sunny day. They all left and I put my younger brother with her brother about fifteen from us at the edge of the woods. We all grew up in the woods so there was nothing any of us didn't know how to deal with if confronted with it. We were well practiced. I just wanted to get this over with but the girl was being timid. She said I'd think she was nuts. I laughed and said that sometimes people don't understand but they need to give it time to sink in. I gained her confidence and so she opened up.

She said, "he" would scare me if I saw him straight on. I said there wasn't much that scared me anymore with three brothers that challenged my life at every turn. She looked worried and said he was special and didn't look like us. Well, I thought he was disfigured or something but no that wasn't it either. I said that sooner or later if I was to talk to this man I'd have to see him in order to understand what he wanted to tell me. I was thinking that maybe there was some wildlife around there that she wasn't familiar with that she couldn't see clearly so it had scared her. No, she said that wasn't it either. She said I had to promise not to look unless he said it was OK. I said I didn't want to be close to him then if I needed to take off in a hurry. She said I couldn't do that because it would upset him. I let out a 'Ha!', and she just gave me a look and said this was very important to her because he'd been very nice to her and been a good friend when she had no others.

Okay, so I appeased her a bit and said I'd play along and be extra nice so I could get this over with. She kept saying not to be alarmed and said she had been the first time she saw him. She said he was very big. I was thinking she must have lost it bad.

I saw movement and there was something looking like a very tall spindly marionette up next to these skinny tall trees. I asked her how she and her siblings had accomplished that. I was laughing but she was looking at me like she had no idea what I was talking about. Then it walked out from the trees without any visible support! I was like okay, there's got to be a sensible explanation to this so I asked if I could move forward after a while to get a better look. I told her I could take this.

Well, she asked him and said he said it was OK. Before that though he wanted to talk to my mind, she said. I thought, oh my God, she's really in 'La La Land,' poor girl, stuck in the sticks of W.Va. and she's lost it! Well, that thing moved again as if shifting from side to side in a standing position. That was human like. I begin to hear this man's voice in my mind and it's conversing with me. It's all like; 'happy to talk to me finally' and 'so excited by my coming to see him' ...I thought I'd caught this girl's insanity and hit myself at the side of my head to shake this voice out of my head.

She asked what was wrong. I told her! She said that was normal. I had news for her but not yet! I had been ordered to see what this was about. This voice seems to be rifling through all my memories like wildfire and then downloading high quality video; like being there in my mind about that bridge falling and other things in the future. I thought my mind was playing tricks on me so I tried to maintain my balance mentally by reminding myself that I was just playing along and this would all play out to be an elaborate hoax.

I inched closer and closer to the edge of this driveway and then a drop off where the bulldozer had shoved the dirt for it. Movement caught my eyes and I looked down to see these big orange bird feet! I thought, oh my God what is that doing in the woods! I took a very slow, very meticulous look up the legs attached to these feet and they looked stork-like. The feet shifted by one picking up and then the other doing it. It was human like in movement but also bird like.

I let my eyes go very slowly up the legs, to the body, ick! And then the chest, also ick! Because I could count the ribs! There appeared to be scant feathers on its skin which was grayish. It was a mix of this bright green color and grayish brown. The more I looked the worse it got but I gritted my teeth and kept my thinking to a minimum. I looked at these wings folded behind its back but yet out a bit to the sides. I could see through them a bit but they looked leathery and stretchy.

I looked at the shoulders which in truth were topped with sharp bumps which I realized were from the wings being folded behind its body. I inadvertently got a good look at its head and a wave of revulsion hit me and I said I was going to just back up slowly to get a better look from a distance. I think it picked up that I was scared of it. I heard it in my mind again and it was upset that I was scared of it. I explained with my mind, crazy as that sounds, just thinking I'd seen some people who were disfigured in my time and this was scary too. I'd just have to get used to it. I did want to get out of there with my life unscathed. This was nuts.

This thing wanted to chat with me and I wanted to go to the bathroom really bad. I told the girl this and she said we'd have to go to the house. He told her, and I heard it too, that he knew I was scared and he was very upset. Then, he got into a part of my mind that showed what I went through at home and somewhere else, a big building in a big city that I didn't remember except in bits. He was livid at me seeing the entire breadth of whatever that was about. I told them both out loud that this wasn't right for this girl or me to be talking to him.

He said his kind didn't want any of them mixing with us because it was dangerous for them. He'd shown me where they were from, and it wasn't this planet. I was feeling dizzy and my brother saw me stagger a bit. I said I had to go and this girl had to help me down to the house, so we were going to leave now and she and I were about to be in big trouble because I wasn't allowed to keep such a secret.

I got out of the woods OK and got up against their garage and wet my pants. Then I felt like I was losing control of my body and was shaking all over. My brother went and got dad. I told him to stay close to the garage because it was out there somewhere and it was huge. He thought I was nuts but I told him sternly that this man that wasn't a man but was a huge creature with wings and big orange feet. He laughed and I said; "I wasn't laughing and we had to get into the house."

We all got into the house and the girl was livid with me for saying I wasn't supposed to tell and now he was angry with her. My head hurt really bad. The adults got their guns out. Phone calls were made and in short order men with guns in pickups and cars came flying into their driveway. Dad wouldn't allow me to tell mom or that woman what I'd seen; no one. I wanted to cry but felt stunned, shocked, very hard. They got me cleaned up and we all sat trying to be quiet. We tried to listen to what was going on.

That was an awful experience. The men went into the woods leaving the women with guns. They soon came back as it was almost dark. We began to see these huge stick looking figures darting past the picture window out front and then the back windows, and the kitchen door and windows. There was more than one of them. All the guns got loaded and we were put into the middle of the house. There was clawing at the roof, siding and windows. This went on for hours and I finally just went to sleep. I was hot and probably in shock so I just went to sleep.

Everything eventually went quiet and it stayed that way for hours. I woke up needing to go to the bathroom. There was a window so someone had to stand there with a gun as I went. Something came to the window and began to claw at it. By then I didn't know what this was or why it was happening. I was given a magazine and put my whole mind on it and read. When I did this all stopped outside. I got tired and quit doing that while wondering what was going on and it began all over again. We could all hear the tin being torn off the roof. I went back to sleep and everything was quiet the rest of what was left of the night.

The next day we packed up and started home. Dad asked before we got to the bridge if we'd be OK crossing it. I looked in my mind and saw it was OK. They wanted to know this over and over again. I was sure. On the Ohio side of the river my brothers and sisters began to talk about what was going on. Something big swooped down at the car and began to claw at it. This happened off and on all the way home. We could hear this thing holding on to the top of the car! Once home I was sent to my room and told to go to sleep. Well, I didn't. I was listening to what they were saying downstairs.

One of my brothers ran downstairs and said there was noise on the roof. Dad told them to go outside and look to see what it was. My brother returned pale looking and said it was a huge bird like thing with glowing red eyes. Dad said that wasn't funny. My brother said he knew it wasn't but this was true. Dad went out and sure enough he came back to say yes it was true. They were all upset and I was up under the roof that was being torn off. My family was watching shingles coming through the air and landing on the ground out back and front. They got the guns out and I was told to lay down and go to sleep. It was OK for a while but then it started again.

My brother came to me and said to look out my window. He told me to look at these little red glowing lights outside. They were eyes. I could see huge spindly wings out there walking around on the ground. It was like they were on their elbows. It was really creepy. Dad took a gun out and then I heard him yell to me saying they were going to hurt him if I didn't say he never hurt me. I said I wasn't allowed to tell lies and he asked me nicely to be nice for him. So, I did. I told them I was OK and I was with my siblings who were older and took care of me. He was scared and we could see several of them near him. We saw him back slowly into the door.

I felt they were in my mind asking what I wanted most in life. I remember thinking I just wanted to run around and have fun like other kids did. I went to sleep and it was quiet until about 2 AM. I woke up to the sound of my older brother's voice asking what we were doing outside with these things and what were they. How did I get outside? My younger brother was behind me and we were running through what I thought was a tunnel on the lawn. I woke up more and saw it was these things lined up with their wings arched over like a tunnel and we'd been running through them!

I was horrified and our older brother saw this. He said dad had sent him out and dad was hanging out the window telling us quietly that it was OK, we weren't in trouble but we should come in because it's really late. I looked at my brothers and asked what was wrong with dad. The older brother said dad was really scared to come outside because those things wanted to hurt him. I asked how he could tell! He laughed a little and said he'd never seen him like this before. He woke him and "asked" for him to go out and get us back in the house. We both dropped our jaws and said; "He asked you?"

We went inside and went right to bed before we got beat for it. We never did and the next day it was like no one wanted to talk about it. My younger brother kept asking what those things were and wasn't it funny that dad was so scared of them. My head hurt. I was diagnosed with traumatic childhood amnesia in 1983 but I have a photographic memory. Okay, so I had no memory of these things until some years later. It was difficult to wrap my head around all of this, still is.

Earlier this year, end of Feb. 2011, I started to again hear the voice of this thing in my mind. It showed me ripples in a pond. I didn't know what that was supposed to be for and I was busy working so I pushed it out of my mind. My mind was being pulled to Middletown, Ohio on the map. I thought OK, what's this about, spit it out. I'm pretty busy these days. No explanation.

This continued and still is happening even now. I was looking at other things about archaeology and information about the thunderbird, dragons, snakes, and how it applies to Native American culture. I'm Shawnee and a direct descendant of Tecumseh. I've still got this unknown 'man' in my mind and he seems to want to chat but I'm thinking these things eat people and people have been known to disappear after seeing these things. I'm thinking I was lucky and blessed to be alive after seeing it that close twice! So, Lon, if you would, say a prayer for me. I'm still very busy with work, photography for home inspections and craft work I have at home. Still from time to time this voice is in my mind. This thing wants to be friends with me but there seems to be something important he wants to convey to me.

I just keep shoving it out of my head. I'm not so sure this thing isn't evil. I mean it did kill a big dog over in W.Va. in 1967. It or they tore it into tiny bits and there wasn't much left of it. If you'd like to turn this into a report I'm sure it would take a lot of work to take out anything that would ID me in any way. I want people to be helped by knowing that these things are real. I can't explain what they are about but I know they are real. Thanks. - DR."

It's interesting to note, that around the same time 'DR' forwarded this account to me, I had just received three Moth-man-like encounter reports from the Cincinnati suburbs. Winged humanoid sightings are not that uncommon along the Ohio River Valley. But rarely has an incident been reported in a metro area, especially within an urban setting. The Chicago sightings are truly unique and historical. I personally doubt that there is a general bad omen associated with these events. But then again, there is an overall consciousness and concern among the population that a malevolent force may be in play.

THERE WAS another disastrous event in which a large flying being was seen prior to the incident. In this instance, the witness believed the winged being was an 'angel', not a portent of caution. I received the following account in 2011:

"Hello sir, a friend referred me to your articles about strange occurrences in West Virginia. The Mothman encounters stirred memories of an incident that took place when I was a girl.

The strange incident took place near Powellton, WV, in December 1934; I was eight years old. At the time, my father worked for Elkhorn-Piney Coal in McDunn. He and the other miners would take a train to the mine each day.

The day before Christmas Eve my father mentioned an unusual sighting he and the others on the train had while traveling back to Powellton from the mine that evening. As they looked out towards the east, they noticed a very large bird flying above the trees. My father was a very simple man and didn't believe in any nonsense but this large bird really caught his attention. He described it as a freakish sized owl very dark in color. The sky was getting dark but they could still make out the large form. He said it also looked at the train as it flew over the trees. Nobody on the train could figure out what it was. The mere fact that my father even mentioned it suggested that it must have been an unusual sight.

My father was scheduled off from work for three days during the Christmas holiday. On December 27, he was getting ready for work but said he felt poorly. My mother was concerned because he had a high fever and awful chills. She insisted he stay home and telephoned the doctor. My father was reluctant on staying home and put up a good argument but my mother was not going to back down. She put him to bed and waited for the doctor.

Well, we waited for hours until the telephone rang. The operator told my mother that the doctor was at McDunn; there had been a horrible train explosion. She couldn't talk but said that the doctor's wife asked her to contact us. My mother was pale when she told my father what had happened. I remember they both started praying and crying. For years both of them thought the large bird was an angel sent by God as a warning and that my father's life was saved for a reason.

My father never went back to the mine. It turned out that he had contracted polio though he was very lucky since he survived it with only a slight limp. We soon moved away to a *small town in Kentucky where my father found the calling and become a Pentecostal preacher. He told his story of survival to anyone who would listen until the day he died.*

I happened to read your stories while looking on the internet with my great-grandson. I always assumed my father saw something more divine. That's what he always believed. I'm not so sure now. Thank you Sir. - Emma."

On December 27, 1934, a boiler in a locomotive hauling mine workers at McDunn in Fayette County, WV exploded, resulting in the death of eighteen miners. Was this sighting a warning by an attendant of God or by an extra-dimensional oracle?

There have been several disasters where witnesses have stated that a large winged being or humanoid had been was seen prior to the incident. For the most part, these revelations are revealed after the fact. But the events leading up to the Chernobyl nuclear disaster may have been noted by witnesses before the eventual explosion and meltdown.

Beginning in early April 1986, the people in and around the little known Chernobyl Nuclear Power Plant began to experience a series of strange events revolving around sightings of a mysterious creature described as a large, dark, and headless man with gigantic wings and piercing red eyes. People affected by this phenomena experienced horrific nightmares, threatening phone calls and first hand encounters with the winged beast which became known as the 'Blackbird of Chernobyl.'

Reports of these strange happenings continued to increase until the morning of April 26, 1986, when at 1:23AM, reactor 4 of the Chernobyl Nuclear Power Plant experienced a catastrophic steam explosion that resulted in a fire which caused a series of additional explosions followed by a nuclear meltdown. The power plant, located near Pripyat, Ukraine, Soviet

Union, spewed a plume of radioactive fallout which drifted over parts of the Western Soviet Union, Eastern and Western Europe, Scandinavia, the UK, Ireland and eastern North America. Large areas of Ukraine, Belarus and Russia were badly contaminated, resulting in the evacuation and resettlement of over 336,000 people.

The workers who survived the initial blast and fire, but would later die of radiation poisoning, claimed to have witnessed what has been described as a large black, bird like creature, with a 20 foot wingspan, gliding through the swirling plumes of irradiated smoke pouring from the reactor. No further sightings of the Black Bird of Chernobyl were reported after the Chernobyl Disaster, leaving researchers to speculate just what haunted the workers of the plant during the days leading up to the disaster.

The most commonly accepted theory suggests that the Black Bird of Chernobyl may have been the same creature spotted in Point Pleasant, West Virginia leading up to the collapse of the Silver Bridge on December 15, 1968. Investigators have suggested that the appearance of this creature is an omen of disasters to come in the area in which it shows itself. The physical description of both the Black Bird of Chernobyl and the Mothman, the creature sighted in West Virginia, are very similar, and the reports of nightmares and threatening phone calls leading up to these disasters are shared in both cases.

A second, less accepted theory, suggests that the Black Bird of Chernobyl was nothing more than the misidentification of the black stork, an endangered species endemic to southern Eurasia. The black stork stands nearly 3 feet tall and has a wing span of nearly 6 feet. This theory however fails to take into account the menacing phone calls and the disturbing nightmares. Also the physical description given by the majority of eyewitnesses who actually saw the Black Bird of Chernobyl does not in any way match the physical appearance of the Black Stork.

Unlike these previous incidents at Point Pleasant and Chernobyl, there doesn't seem to be any instances of strange phone calls or nightmares associated with the Chicago sightings.

20

WHAT DO PEOPLE THINK ABOUT THE SIGHTINGS?

THROUGHOUT THE INVESTIGATION, I have kept tabs on the public opinion in regards to the Chicago Phantom sightings. I wanted to know what people thought about the origin and identity of these beings, as well as any reasonable leads that they may be able to offer:

> *"First off, I love your work, and Phantoms & Monsters. I am very interested/intrigued by all the reports this year, especially how many there have been. As to what the Phantoms(s) are, I'm not certain. But I don't think they are 'harbingers of doom.' Personally I think the one at Point Pleasant in the 60s, was not connected to the bridge collapse directly. No idea why it has picked Chicago, but I think they are either extraterrestrial beings, as there was a rarely mentioned Mothman report in Hythe, Kent, UK in 1963 (about 15 miles from where I live), and the witnesses saw a UFO first, then a short while later, came face to face with the Mothman, so it could have been 'dropped off' as it were, for reasons unknown.*
>
> *They may be inter-dimensional beings that have somehow made their way through to our dimension. Either a portal is*

not being sufficiently guarded against this happening, or it is damaged. It could be being manipulated somehow, so as to let them in, to our dimension. As to who could be doing this, is anyone's guess. I think there are three different ones, going by report description/artists impressions.

The frustrating part of all this, is the lack of photo/video evidence, especially how often we use them. I'm hoping the photos that have been taken by some other witnesses, as mentioned in your reports, find their way to you, as I'd love to see one. It is a subject, both fascinating, and terrifying.

You've said on your site that you remote view. Have you thought of using co-ordinates, of any of the dates/times in question, to maybe find out what it is? You might get some idea if they are positive/negative, and how/why they are here. - Clive."

There has been an attempt to remote view these incidents, but so far very little useful information has been obtained. A future series of sessions are being planned through the use of two separate groups.

Any pertinent results gathered from those sessions will be used in the investigation.

"I am positive these beings do exist. So many other people feel the way I do as well. There have been reports for a very long time now, and I am glad there are people like yourself, interested and publishing this information. There is definitely something going on.

Where do they come from? Do they come from other worlds or UFOs? Do they live amongst us as another animal species? I have thought about this many times. I know and believe that this is all very real. There seems to be many different species witnessed in various parts of the world.

Regarding most of the accounts, I believe these people, for the most part, have no reason to lie. They shouldn't be ridiculed.

Why Chicago? I'm not sure. It seems almost as though they want to be seen. Maybe they're growing in numbers. It may be a perfect habitat along the Great Lakes. Most seem to look bat-like with humanoid features. And I will admit, I've seen the same thing back in 2005, near Milwaukee, and so I believe.

I'm thankful others have also had these experiences. It makes me feel not so alone with this. With so many negative people out there, it's something you generally keep to yourself. I'm also thankful for this forum, and group. - Deb S."

There have been a few unconfirmed reports of similar flying humanoids in the Milwaukee area, during the same period of time as the Chicago sightings. The Great Lakes, in particular Lake Michigan, has a long history of bizarre and unexplained activity. We have taken that fact under consideration throughout the investigation.

"I don't know what to make of this Mothman phenomenon. I personally think it's on par with the 'Mothman Prophecies.' I believe it shows itself to warn of something bad in the future for Chicago. I do think there is more than one, although it could be a shapeshifting Mothman.

It's very intriguing. As a twenty-seven year Chicago resident I've never heard of anything like this until I saw the post about the Oz Park sighting. And now, each day I find myself looking up and around the skies of Chicagoland. I work three to four blocks from the Schiller St. encounter and I pass that intersection every day. It's so very creepy. I can't decide if I want to see this thing or not. The Mothman cometh. - Daniel A."

During the months of July and August 2017, I received approximately twenty telephone calls per day from Chicago residents who wondered aloud if these sightings were a warning of impending doom. People are sincerely terrified by these reports. I tried my best to dispel their fears as best as I could.

"I suspect that it may be a type of semi-corporeal intelligence(s) that can possibly take various forms, or even appear differently to different people. Witnesses' descriptions, points of view, emotions at the time of an experience, etc., may naturally vary as well, much like witnesses to a crime. I have doubts that it's always present in a physical form.

Is it something that feeds off of emotional energy? Is it somehow attracted to the Chicago area in particular due to the abnormally high homicide rate, and the trauma/energies/emotions around that? Does it/they feed off of the emotions of fear and/or awe of witnesses? Is it something that was somehow purposely 'summoned'?

I know there are more questions than opinions, but these are my thoughts. In many reported instances, the entity seems to want to be noticed. I'm sure my thoughts on this are not original.

Thanks for all of your hard work. - Jim."

Jim definitely thinks like an anomalies investigator; and we have been thinking along the same lines. If these beings are semi-corporeal and able to take on different forms, then it's going to be a tough nut to crack. I believe that emotional energy exuded by living humans can generate or perpetuate certain entities, and it's a theory we are deeply exploring.

"I get the impression that they are intelligent beings and not just some unknown animal. Can someone, therefore, calmly

try and make contact with these being(s)? You must exercise extreme caution, as we do not know these beings' origin, purpose or their attitude towards us. The humming sound witnesses hear and feel, could be an audible communication medium used by these beings. My opinion is that they study us and try to instigate communication from time to time with witnesses.

Since we are human, we get scared out of our wits at anything that is strange and doesn't fit our view of existence and thus miss opportunities to gain knowledge that might help or even save us; while at the same time we gain possible friends/"allies." Kind regards. - CRR."

That's an interesting perspective, though enabling communication with these beings may be something best initiated by a linguistics expert, and only under certain safe conditions. None of the witnesses I talked to were in any state conducive to intelligent interaction.

"The Chicago Phantom is fascinating on so many levels. First, I have evolved into believing that entities like the Phantom, Bigfoot, Dogman, etc. are very likely inter-dimensional creatures. They are so enigmatic that we can really only venture wild theories. In fact, the deeper I get involved in cryptids, UFO's and the unexplained. I realize that the latter category says it all. This stuff is not even close to being explained.

So why has the Phantom chosen Chicago to make his appearance? I have no clue, but the association of the Mothman with the bridge collapse leads me in that direction. Is it possible that a calamity awaits the Windy City? Honestly, I have no idea, but all these sightings sure are fascinating. I'm certain that those witnesses who have gotten a *close look are deeply affected, at least I would be. My UFO sighting of a couple of years ago never leaves my head, I'll tell you that.*

Our world is positively filled with the unexplained and I can only wonder if we'll learn more in the next life. Who knows? Thanks again for what you do. - Murray R."

I believe there is an inter-dimensional aspect to these winged humanoids. I also believe that we are a part of other realities that parallel our earth plane. Could these beings have a natural existence in one of these parallel worlds?

"I have reviewed the data with friends and we all concur that we think it's a highly sophisticated prank; an ingenious drone built to giant specifications (seven feet or more). The Mothman drone, apparently, never lets itself get close enough to eyewitnesses for definitive details to be observed about its countenance. I imagine the drone operator has a few hearty guffaws every time he/she reads the responses of the eyewitnesses.

I suspect that these reports will continue for a while until such time the operator gets tired of doing this or the truth is uncovered as to what the Mothman actually is. To the best of my knowledge with such a plethora of reports coming in, none of the major, local TV stations such as CBS, NBC and ABC have reported on these sightings. Maybe they know something about this that the general public doesn't? Regards. - Joe."

Everybody is entitled to their own opinions, but the means and assets needed in order to pull off a stunt of this proportion would be a bit too ambitious in my opinion. It's a better theory than stating that a Giant Blue Heron with bright red eyes and the ability to suddenly accelerate upwards from a standing position is showing itself throughout the city and suburbs; but not by much.

"I have spent a great deal of time listening to podcasts, reading and listening to interviews about various phenomena from around the world in concerning humanoid-type beings. I've been focusing mainly on current encounters that people have been having in forests and urban areas and I've come to a few conclusions about them.

I think that throughout history humans have had encounters with creatures that are often relegated to folklore status. I think that before the advent of the internet there may have been a great number of creature sightings that were subject to the local customs and religious beliefs in areas around the globe. For instance, if a small village of aboriginal people see a Sasquatch they may hold veneration for the creature whereas someone from a larger city center may be traumatized and horrified at the idea of a "monster" roaming in the woods. With two different perspectives comes two different ways of dealing with an issue.

For instance it may be such common knowledge, in certain parts of the world, that strange creatures exist that when someone speaks of them they are not seen as insane or naive. If however, a person in "civilized" society mentions anything that is paranormal or unusual they are mocked and shamed, much the same way as the Salem Witches.

I mean, back when we didn't have knowledge of what people in other countries were actually doing and thinking, other than what the media told us, we were pretty isolated in our social bubbles everywhere around the globe. So now, with the internet, we have the ability to see what other people think and experience from their perspectives rather than through the eye of the media: it's more personal and perhaps less biased, at times. Now we can read and hear what other people have been experiencing outside the sphere of what the media has been covering all these years and perhaps that right there has something to do with these sightings. (Read on, it will make more sense soon).

So we get back to the 'Mothman,' as I'll refer to it. What if these creatures have always been around? I mean, what if they have been showing themselves to people but not so much in urban areas. What if there have been a load of sightings over a stretched-out period of time, but because there was nowhere for people to report them, people just ignored and eventually forgot about them? Add to this the fact that people are generally lazy and if they don't have a direct line to a reporting service then their sightings were dismissed and eventually forgotten?

Before the modern age of machines, people's main focus in life was survival and religion so anything outside of that, like flying monsters, would be dismissed outright. I am aware that the original 'Mothman' sightings took place before the internet but there were great numbers of people who saw this thing (or things) so it's understandable that it would be reported in the news and talked about for years that followed. So the point I am making is that I believe these types of creatures and many more have been around forever. I don't think they are anything new. Whether or not they have been seen in cities as much as they have in Chicago, as of late, is not known for sure. I'm noticing that there seems to be a great number of experiences with all types of unexplained creatures from all around the world lately. Part of that, obviously, is because of the internet allowing for easier communication and access to research sources on topics of this nature.

From all that I've been reading and hearing, on the topic of bizarre creatures, it seems as if there is a bit of an uptick in *sightings and experiences with paranormal creatures, lately. Again, I'm not sure if it's just because more people are making reports, because they feel safe to do so on the internet, or because there really is a surge in strange occurrences.*

I'm wondering if the increase in sightings of unusual creatures has to do with a planetary consciousness shift. Perhaps, we've turned a corner in our mental and spiritual evolution and these creatures know this. Perhaps they have been revealing themselves over a long period of time but now things have ramped-up a bit in our psyches enabling them to reveal more to us. Perhaps we are slowly being opened up subconsciously to what they are trying to reveal to us. Maybe creatures like Sasquatch, Mothman, and all the other strange creatures, are aware of our human spiritual evolution and this current explosion of sightings is guiding us through initial stages of this evolution. The 1960s Mothman sightings were possibly a primer as the creatures knew they would become part of our folklore thus opening the door for future interactions leading to a full disclosure at some time in the future. Maybe they will come back again in 10 or 20 years, or sooner, depending on our level of mental progress.

I don't buy into the thought that these things are devils or evil. I mean, I don't know for sure but I strongly suspect that they are here to monitor us as well as guide us by forcing us to challenge our beliefs. I think they know that if a ton of them showed up all over the planet and tried to sort us all out at once that we would retaliate with violence as we are not ready to have the complete truth revealed to us yet. Baby steps.

This leads me to believe that because they are terrifying to look at that we have projected negative beliefs onto these creatures based on the fact that we have polarized views of good and evil. It seems as if they are trying to be seen by us and perhaps they are planting some sort of physic seed in our brains just by allowing us to see them. I think these creatures are complex beings from another level of existence that are here to show us something that we aren't able to grasp yet. When that one Mothman creature stopped in front of that couple, just mere feet away, and hovered, that tells me that the creature was trying to communicate with them and leave an impression with them. It obviously wasn't trying to attack them but wanted them to have a strong tale to tell the other humans.

The "vibrating legs" gives me an indication that perhaps it emits some sort of sound wave that is consciously undetectable to humans (I could be reaching here). I would be very curious to know if that couple is having communication dreams or other strange types of occurrences at home, since that incident. Will you be following up with them?

This brings me to something else. I have become very open and aware in the last 10 years how much our natural human insight and knowledge has been suppressed. I realize now that we have had a reality built for us as a means to control our senses and beliefs which has skewed much of our natural curiosity about the natural world. Since becoming aware of this, I have started to search for the truth about who we are and what our true purpose is. So when I hear about Bigfoot, Dogman, Mothman, UFOs or anything else of this nature, I don't see bizarre phenomena but rather doorways to the truth.

There's so much to explore about reality and I think the first step in our evolution would be to shed our fear of the unknown. Beyond fear lies a bigger reality than we could ever have imagined and as I often say, humans are more powerful and immense than what we've been lead to believe and it's time we find out the truth. Thanks for reading. Cheers. - Betty G."

I couldn't have stated it better myself. I have been a paranormal and Fortean researcher for almost forty years, and when a tangible shift in the collective consciousness occurs, you sense it. I do believe that the internet is partly responsible for more open-minded thinking. But I also believe that people are beginning to realize that life is more than dogma and routine. You can call it 'enlightenment' or maybe 'esoteric awareness,' but there has been a palpable conversion to learning and living beyond the standard. For that, I thank the Angels each and every day.

"From the descriptions, I've come up with the idea that it is a humanoid with some kind of "wings" and reflective eyes. I say that because I've spent a huge amount of hours on sea-going cryptids and from eyewitness descriptions it's clear to me that while people may all be seeing the same creature, they perceive things differently because of their background/perspective and knowledge base. People have reported Nessie as having a dog's head, a horse's head, sheep's head, giraffe antlers, etc.

I think the same holds true here. People see something outside their library of knowledge and make best guesses based on their individual abilities to apply the known to the unknown.

With the Chicago Phantom, it is clearly humanoid in size and shape and does have wings of some sort. However, in more than one instance people have reported the being launching into the air and then mentioning the wings. It's not like a bird that uses its momentum from its wings as it launches into the air. This thing, from at least a couple of the accounts, launched into the air and then the wings spread. This leads me to think the wings are for stabilization and not necessarily for propulsion.

As to the nature of the being, it is localized for some reason. The range of sightings keeps it centered on the coastal edge of the lake. I think if it was something government related, as in technology, it would show up in a variety of places to keep patterns from emerging, so people couldn't anticipate it.

The fact that it's staying centered in one locale means to me that it's an independent being. In recent years I've come to put a lot more stock in the idea of parallel worlds and us being in contact with things other than our own world. Like Mothman, there are instances where I think we have intrusions into our world by other beings.

I think that whatever the Chicago Phantom is, it's not a simple animal which is being misidentified, nor something military. I don't have a clue what its intentions might be, though maybe time will tell. I will be curious to see whether something happens like in the Mothman case, or if it just suddenly quits and we never see it again. - Craig C."

This narrative makes a good point; different people have varying perspectives as to what they are seeing. Overall, the sighting descriptions have been fairly consistent. But I have wondered if the posted reports may have influenced any of the later witnesses. For instance, the descriptions of the wing shape. Most of the witnesses, since May 2017, have described the wing as resembling that of a bat and that it had leathery skin. Did the witnesses actually observe that, or was it an imprint from previous sighting reports? I may be over thinking in these regards, but it is just another part of the investigative process that causes me to pause and consider.

"As a student of John Keel's work, I cannot help wonder what devious fate awaits Chicago, especially in a time with mass shootings seemingly happening once a week. This phenomenon is currently unfolding, the likes of which have

not happened perhaps since the original sightings in Point Pleasant. Rarely is an event unfolding before us with so many current Ufologists, Cryptozoologists, paranormal investigators at the ready, but many seem to be dismissive of these events.

It almost seems like a flap, series-of-events, what have you, has to be vetted and long over before serious research of it can begin. MUFON has been dismissive, Loren Coleman has chalked a lot of Chicago's sightings up to hysteria, and Seth Breedlove defers to you instead of providing an opinion. I can't help but wonder why these encounters are receiving such abysmal prominence by today's researchers, save for you and your team.

It certainly is a popular topic amongst paranormal podcasts, but everyone seems to be deferring to you instead of sinking their teeth in. I feel two fold about this; it says a lot about your stature amongst researchers and investigators. You are held in high regard and I am sure many are thinking; "Oh, Lon's on this, cool. He'll figure it out or at least keep everyone updated." And second, I feel, researchers have been caught off guard by these unprecedented events.

Many recent, insurmountable cases such as Stan Romanek, the Polybius conspiracy, BEKs, the Hat Man, etc. have been exceptionally researched but have been easily digestible, i.e., "Stan's a hoaxer, Polybius is an urban legend, BEKs happen to 'other' people, Hat Man is just a shadow person." But for the Chicago Phantom, much like its big brother, the Mothman, nobody knows what to make of it. Even a hypothesis is vague at best. The complexity of Mothman appears to be enduring in 2017. How amazing. - Nomar S."

I can't honestly explain why other investigators are seemingly uninterested or that they'd rather defer the sightings to me and the Task Force. The fact that these sightings are occurring in an urban and populated environment may have something to do with the hesitation. It may be true that people will become more interested in the phenomenon after it has ceased and out of the public eye. I'm not willing to sit back and ignore the opportunity. If others wish to discount the sightings or tell enthusiasts to contact me, then so be it.

21

CHICAGO PHANTOM TASK FORCE - SUMMATIONS

IT HAS BEEN an honor working with the Chicago Phantom Task Force, a fine group of seasoned investigators and researchers. I asked the members of the Task Force and a few colleagues, who are familiar with the sightings, to write a summation for this book; including their personal thoughts and theories:

MANUEL NAVARETTE:

"The 2017 Chicago flap is truly monumental and a boon to both researchers and naysayers alike.

The amount of data collected from the sightings far exceeds any of the data collected during the Point Pleasant, West Virginia sightings. Starting with the first sighting in Oz Park and winding-down with the rash of sightings in Little Village, no other group of flying humanoid sightings can compare in both variety and composition. An investigative team from multiple paranormal research associations grouped up in an unprecedented move to form the Chicago Phantom Task Force and tackled the reports and collection of data as a single unit. It's a move that hasn't been done before and quite frankly may never be done again. As of the writing of this summary, it has been over 1 month since the last reported sighting and likely that the sightings may be coming to an end.

After I reviewed the information provided, starting from the first sighting back in March until the last sighting in November, I have come to the conclusion that the witness accounts were valid. There has been no tangible evidence of hoaxing.

I feel that this entity was a flesh-and-blood entity and that it was seen on multiple occasions throughout the city of Chicago during the summer of 2017. It is also my experienced opinion that the City of Chicago was well aware of the sightings, as documented by multiple city workers, some of them from within City Hall itself. And I feel the City of Chicago took obvious steps to conceal the sightings and to keep the information away from of the media's attention; possibly to save face and protect the city from loss of tourism dollars. There has been a good deal of empirical evidence gathered in order to backup this statement.

I also feel that certain entities went out of their way to come up with some of the most absurd and asinine theories in order to debunk the phenomenon. Despite many of these outrageous claims, that includes Great Blue Herons, two ships out on the lake and designer kites, the sheer amount of anecdotal evidence gathered from all over the city and surrounding areas points to a very real phenomenon.

I fully support the premise that there were multiple entities seen at various locations in the metro area. The working theories of an opening of a portal or gateway from an alternate reality, as well as the possibility of a summoning, *give credence to the sheer amount of sightings from a variety of witnesses throughout the region.*

As to what was seen in the skies over Chicago during the summer of 2017; I cannot give you a definite answer. I could give you a couple of personal thoughts, all of which are based on the evidence in hand. In my opinion, there were multiple entities involved, possibly of different species. I sense that some of these entities were brought forward intentionally, although for what purpose has not been revealed. Whatever the reason was, it seems like the entities we're not meant to harm anyone; possibly as a means to scare them. Could this have been an undiscovered species? Perhaps it is. But until more evidence is gathered that points to this prospect, it will remain in the realm of speculation.

In closing, I feel very honored to have been part of the Task Force that investigated these sightings, and I wish to personally thank each and every one of them for not only being professionals, but for becoming great friends and colleagues.

I feel that there is a likelihood that future reports may begin once the weather becomes warmer and more people are out and about. Rest assured to that once those calls start coming in, the Chicago Phantom Task Force will stand ready to investigate, in an attempt to find answers to what was in the skies over Chicago during 2017."

Manuel Navarette is a friend and colleague, who immediately contacted me when the Oz Park encounter was initially reported. He was steadfastly involved with all aspects of the Chicago Phantom investigation, personally interviewing many of the witnesses. He is an experienced UFO investigator and researcher, reporting on the phenomenon for many years at UFOClearinghouse.com

TOBIAS WAYLAND:

"I don't hate cranes. Rather, I hate what cranes represent. They've been the go to explanation used by debunkers for flying humanoids since at least 1966, and it irritates me to no end that here we are in 2017 and they're the featured explanation for anyone looking to dismiss what's happening in Chicago. The worst part, though, for me, is that cranes probably could explain a few sightings; and that's the problem with investigation. We have this tendency to want one blanket explanation for everything, and we want it to be our explanation; the one we were hoping for. And, after a while, we start looking at a flap of sightings as one large case, rather than many smaller ones. We begin to lose our ability to see the forest for the trees, as it were; and sometimes we mistake the whole forest for something else entirely.

It's a danger we can't afford. We've got to look at each reported sighting and judge it on its own merits. On the subject of cranes, for instance, let's examine the Calumet Park sightings. These sightings took place within a week of each other, and they both involved fathers spending time with their sons in the early evenings around dusk.

The witnesses described a large, black, winged being with a roughly humanoid shape. But one of them also reported hearing; "Something that sounded like train brakes when the train [sic] slowing down," which, if you've ever heard a crane, is a pretty good description of what they sound like. And they're big. I wouldn't fault someone for a second who saw one and thought its wingspan was ten feet—that's only a couple of feet off from their actual size.

Cranes often have seven to eight-foot wingspans. These

large birds fly with their legs out behind them, and could conceivably be mistaken for a flying humanoid. Consider that a bird in flight, backlit by the setting sun, would appear black, and it becomes a pretty good explanation. I can't say for sure that they saw a crane in flight, but it makes a certain amount of sense. I think a misidentified bird works as an explanation for many of the sightings that consist merely of some large flying creature being seen briefly in the late evening or early nighttime, and if that's all this flap consisted of, then that would likely be the end of it for me; but it's not, so it isn't.

Take the Oz Park sighting. There's no way, if you believe the witness, that it can be explained away by any mundane animal. And there's no reason, at this point, not to believe her. I know that not everyone agrees with that assessment, but I have yet to see any evidence that would lead me to doubt her veracity. And there have been dozens of similarly bizarre sightings in Illinois going back years. Each one, taken on its own merits, is unexplainable if you believe the witness.

I had a conversation with the Illinois State Director of the Mutual UFO Network (MUFON), Sam Maranto, at the 2017 Milwaukee Paranormal Conference, and he insisted that someone is running what he called an "op" surrounding these sightings. I assume that's an abbreviation for operation; at least that's what it seemed like in the context of our conversation. In any case, he told me, speaking very quickly and emphatically, that somebody—be they the government or internet pranksters —is hoaxing these sightings.

But what about people like Lon, Manuel, or, to a lesser degree, myself, who have spoken to witnesses? Well, we're apparently being fooled, you see. Mr. Maranto was very concerned for our credibility, and advised me that MUFON had traced several of the reports back to the same Chicago-area IP address. But it's not unusual for people in a metropolitan city like Chicago to share an IP address, and many of the reports come from the same, specific sections of the city; all of which makes it a little more likely that it's just a coincidence.

And the idea that everybody else working on the case is just too dumb to know that the people to whom they are speaking directly are con artists, well, I find that just slightly less offensive than the idea that all any of the witnesses saw was cranes. There isn't any comfortable blanket explanation under which all of these sightings can rest, and it seems to me the people trying to find one are doing so out of loyalty to their own beliefs and not the truth.

I didn't know Lon at all when I started covering this case for The Singular Fortean Society, but it only took the first feature interview I did with him to convince me that he certainly wasn't making anything up, and he doesn't seem like a man who has much interest in being fooled. It is also my understanding that Mr. Maranto has had very limited contact with any of the witnesses—in fact, MUFON wasn't even able to contact the witnesses who originally sent in the three sightings in April that peaked my, along with many other's, interest in this flap in the first place. I understand the temptation to disbelieve the testimony being collected, I really do; and I further understand how difficult it can be to have to accept the testimony secondhand. But I also understand the witnesses' requests for anonymity, and I challenge anyone who doubts the honesty or motivation of those investigating this case to actually speak to the investigators; you'll find them very approachable.

I've collected my share of strange sightings and weird experiences since becoming more involved in investigating Chicago's flying humanoid. I've spoken to a young man in Rockford who had an encounter with a bat-winged creature and an old truck that came straight out of Jeepers Creepers, *and a witch in Chicago who's concerned a summoning ritual she performed in 2015 could be at least partially responsible for the current sightings.*

I've had email and social media contact with many, many more this past year, too, some of whom made it into the timeline of events and some who did not. The people with whom I've talked have myriad theories regarding what's behind their sightings; a mundane animal, previously undiscovered species, inter-dimensional interloper, or supernatural being were some of the most popular. But the one thing they all had in common was a certain sincerity, and the total lack of desire to profit from their sighting in any way.

So, in reading these reports, I hope you'll do a few things: stay open-minded, don't assume the worst out of anybody involved unless they give you a reason, and please, try to see the forest for the trees."

Tobias Wayland is a passionate Fortean and outspoken paranormal agnostic who graduated from the University of Wisconsin-Madison. He's spent the last nine years actively investigating the unusual; for the first five years as a MUFON field investigator, and the last four independently. His years as an investigator have served him best by illustrating that when it comes to the anomalous, the preternatural, and the paranormal, any answers he's found are still hopelessly outnumbered by questions. He is a member of the Chicago Phantom Task Force and his writings can be found on his website at www.Singular-Fortean.com

TIMOTHY RENNER:

"One of the most difficult positions to take is the position of no-position, by saying, "I do not know." It tends to frustrate people. People want answers and look to researchers, authors, podcast creators, and the like as "experts." We may be able to rattle on about famous cases, witness reports, and all manner of evidence, but any solutions we provide to the mysteries of the paranormal boil down to theories. Some researchers may even loudly proclaim that they have "figured it all out." Most often this means they are exhausted and frustrated with all of the questions surrounding the paranormal and they have come to the dull and oft-repeated conclusion that every paranormal entity is "a demon." The longer I am involved in paranormal/Fortean research, the more I find myself saying, "I don't know." Such it is with the cases at hand.

My preferred method of investigation is a combination of research and experience. I really like to put "boots on the ground," to be on-site, observe, and add my own notes and possible experiences to those of the witnesses. Due to distance and time constraints I was usable to get to the Chicago area. Being a member of the Chicago Phantom Task Force, however, was quite literally the next best thing. Task Force members did put boots on the ground, visited every sighting location, interviewed witnesses, and relayed the details back to the Task Force, often in as close to real-time as possible.

The sheer number of sightings was extremely impressive. This caused some other researchers to lash out and claim we were somehow making up stories and witnesses; an accusation that seemed to be based on nothing more than their lack of access to these witnesses. In this field, witnesses do not come forward lightly; it is often with the promise of anonymity that witnesses speak at all. Researchers are not obliged to share witnesses; but having a view from the inside I can say no one in this task force was making up stories or witnesses. There were enough reports coming in legitimately; enough, "inside baseball." so to speak that we were asked to provide our theories and to clarify my, "I don't know" from above, I will add these thoughts:

This is the highest concentration of paranormal sightings in regards to quantity over time and geographic area of which I have ever been aware. This may be because the internet allows for a flow of information that wouldn't have been possible when the Mothman was haunting Point Pleasant, for instance; or during the Pennsylvania

Bigfoot/UFO flap of 1973-1974.

Still, the Chicago Phantom sightings are extremely impressive. I am not sure these sightings spell "doom" for Chicago as many suppose (based on Mothman sightings as precursors to tragedy, ala Point Pleasant). Cryptid sightings, of all sorts, seem to be increasing. As fewer people go out into nature and experience the unknown of the wilderness; where, in the past, we were met by faeries, goblins, spectres, and hairy wild-men of all sorts. The "other" may be looking for new ways to reach us. Whatever cryptid creatures are; and again, I will play my "I don't know" card here; they seem to need to be seen as much as we need to see them. We can turn our backs on the wilderness, but the unknown will still come calling. Right into our cities. Right into Chicago."

Timothy Renner is an illustrator, author, and folk musician living in Pennsylvania. His illustrations have appeared in the pages of various books, magazines, fanzines and comics as well as on many record and CD covers. Since 1995, Timothy has been making music both solo and with his band, Stone Breath. Stone Breath has released over a dozen albums. Timothy's first book, 'Beyond the Seventh Gate' was published in 2016, with his second; 'Bigfoot in Pennsylvania' following in 2017.

Timothy is the co-host of Strange Familiars, a podcast concerning the paranormal, weird history, folklore and the occult. He makes regular appearances on the paranormal radio show; *Where Did the Road Go?*, and has appeared as a guest on many other podcasts and radio programs, including *Coast to Coast AM*. Find Timothy at: www.StrangeFamiliars.com

---

SEAN FORKER:

"Since we've been following these sightings of a strange flying being in Chicago, I've wondered to myself, both internally and vociferously, as to what we are dealing with. This Phantom / Being / whatever we want to call it; is it even of our world? Confounded, I cannot seem to ascertain what it wants from us. Does it want to be seen? Does it know it's being seen? Is it aware of its insurgence in our time and space? Why has it not attempted to contact us? Does it carry a message?

In Point Pleasant, West Virginia, when a similar being, the 'Mothman' was sighted, it was followed by a major calamity; the collapse of the Silver Bridge. So far, there have not been any incidents of disaster befalling on Chicago. It's been almost a year since this recent 'sightings flap' started. Almost certainly something would have happened by now, if this entity would have been a harbinger of sorts.

Following this scenario, I feel at this point our creature, this entity, is not a harbinger.

Personally, I feel justified by eliminating the sightings as a hoax. I don't think we are the victims of a conspiracy to pull some investigators into a stupid prank. These witnesses all seem genuine with no pretense. There is no personal gain, as we have not identified witnesses publicly. Their stories seem *within reason, with no grand payoff with no embellishment. These are everyday folks just going about their everyday lives, with a brief encounter of something peculiar. I would expect far more adventurous stories if these were hoaxes.*

I guess if I was to chalk this up to something, perhaps it falls into the emerging category of 'Ultra-terrestrial.' This may be an entity not from our time or space. Perhaps it is something new. Who says we have any answers as to what this is? This is some serious John Keel sh*t. - Sean Forker."

Sean Forker is a seasoned Bigfoot / paranormal investigator, based in north central Pennsylvania. He is a close colleague and friend, and has been involved in many cases with me. Sean, Butch Witkowski and I investigate as part of several research groups, including Phantoms & Monsters Fortean Research, the UFO Research Center of Pennsylvania, Pennsylvania Lycan Investigations and the Keystone Bigfoot Project. We also host Arcane Radio together.

VANCE NESBITT:

"As the history papers have been written and the theories penned, we still have no more solid evidence as what hundreds have witnessed in this seemingly normal world. A man-sized creature with a membrane bat-like wings and large glowing red or orange eyes sounds much like something manifested from the mind of H.P. Lovecraft or a story shared on the 'Twilight Zone.' How could it be that such a diverse group of eyewitnesses to such a being stand organized to produce a mass hoax? None of them are familiar with each other let alone not even introduced to each other. Yet the phenomenon

of such a profound encounter with a flying humanoid may seem science fiction but stands alone as not science fiction at all.

Ask any witness to re-tell their tale and the emotion seems to come back to the surface in a very unsettling way.

I have tried like every researcher in the cryptid community to find a link or a shred of evidence to begin building a foundation of discovery as to the 'What and Why' of this creature known as the Mothman.

A summation of a possibility is one I have shared in the past. Most all of us have found ourselves lost in a large structure or a road journey that leaves us with that dread of fear of never finding our way back out. The frustration and irritation at the time causes us to act out of the normal behavior that we feel is being our normal self even though it may only last for a few uncomfortable moments. I personally draw the comparison of letting a fly into your home by accidental means. There clearly is an aggressive campaign undertaken by the fly to find its way back out to its familiar environment. It's not its normal behavior to have interaction with us by the annoying buzzing around our head and repeated attacks of bouncing along the clear barrier of a window. The fly is instinctively looking for a way out.

Perhaps the events in Chicago are a representation of such behavior by a creature that found its way into our earthly home and is in ever desperation to find its way back to the environment it is familiar with. Perhaps the aggressive actions are more out of fear than evil intent. The observation by such a being may see us as a bipedal threat first. Humans are by nature a violent species.

So what if the creature is mundane, normal in its population but found its way here through a doorway we have yet to discover? What if the aggressive stylings of this cryptid *are rather a domination instinct out of nothing more than fear and survival? Asking more questions may help to narrow down what not to ask later on, but for now, I feel we are dealing with something that only the limits of our minds may try to understand. There may also be that far reach outside the box that would sound so ridiculous that the skeptics would take it only as fuel for their own agenda.*

I hope that the current events in Chicago lead us to perhaps one answer rather than nothing at all. - Vance Nesbitt."

Vance Nesbitt is the host of the Caravan of Lore radio show. Through the years of life experiences he has always found the paranormal subject matter compelling. It wasn't until his late twenties that the subject became reality with personal experiences of the unexplained. Since then he has worked in aviation and has taken flight in rare aircraft of previous wars. In this era of his life he dedicates time to his love of artwork through painting and visual stimuli. Vance is currently honing the skills of communication with the attentive audience worldwide in the subject of all things paranormal.

NICOLE TITL GRAJEK:

"It's been extremely interesting to be part of the task force investigating the Chicago Mothman sightings this year. I believe that the abundance of Chicago phantom sightings occurring this year have a connection with the meteor that landed in Lake Michigan on February 6, 2017. Approximately one month later, sightings started occurring in the Chicago area. The connection with the meteor is not

known, but I believe there are several beings of unknown origin.

My background is mostly with paranormal research so I don't know much about cryptids. However, due to the large number of sightings and the distances between the locations, it appears that there are two or more creatures. It seems like this creature in 2017 is following water sources to navigate the city going down the Calumet River and Chicago River to Lake Michigan and lingering around there. All of these water sources intertwine and connect with each other. It is in various parts of the city and not sticking to one location. It is interesting to note that later on in the summer, sightings occurred in the outer suburbs 40 miles or so from downtown Chicago, perhaps suggesting that this creature was traveling around. Once again, due to the numerous waterways, it would be extremely easy to navigate around the environment if the waterways served as a home and/or portal for these creatures with Lake Michigan being ground zero."

Nicole Tito Grajek grew up on the southside of Chicago surrounded by many ghost stories, especially the infamous Resurrection Mary and Bachelor's Grove tales. She pursued an undergraduate education at Benedictine University earning a major in biology and a minor in psychology. From there, she went on to Northwestern University, obtaining her doctorate in physical therapy.

Nicole enjoys performing EVP sessions at various locations and has been able to travel around the country with fellow teammates as part of the American Spectral Society. Her EVP partner, Lisa Krick, and she operate a website that showcases some great audio evidence from around the country. www.Ghostly-Voices.com

ALBERT S. ROSALES:

"Back in the late 6os; 1966-67 to be exact, Point Pleasant, West Virginia had its winged humanoid, or the 'Mothman' as it was named by the great Fortean researcher John Keel (born; Alva John Kiehl).

The encounters of this winged anomaly were accompanied by other strange phenomena, UFOs, mutilations, MIB's, etc. It was later said to have been an omen to the terrible tragedy in December 1967 when the Silver Bridge, which crossed the Ohio River into Point Pleasant, suddenly collapsed on December 15, 1967, killing 46 people (two of the victims were never found). However the sightings of the Mothman did not really end. There were sporadic encounters later, through the 70s and 80s and later.

Now in the first half of the Twenty-first Century, a winged mystery has descended on Chicago, Illinois. This historic city, with its violent past, is no stranger to all kinds of bizarre phenomena. But our focus is the recent events so diligently chronicled by my friend and researcher Lon Strickler in his Phantoms & Monsters blog.

There were strange events and encounters before August of 2016; in the Chicago suburb of Cicero (Al Capone's headquarters back in gangland Chicago) when a man saw a large winged humanoid perched on a lamp post. Events took off around February 2017 and have not stopped as of November, here are dozens of encounters all chronicled by Lon. Some witnesses called the entity a "man-bat" and others a "black devil" or a "winged man" etc. Whatever it is, it has given some of those witnesses a sense of 'evil' or foreboding.

Unlike Point Pleasant there haven't been too many other associated events, like UFOs, etc (that I am aware).

There has been worldwide interest in these events, and Fortean and UFOs groups as far as Russia have been keeping a close watch on the incident, publishing their encounters in their own blogs and newsletters.

Lon has remained open-minded and thorough in his investigation of these bizarre events. I can only conjecture as the origin of the "man-bat." Is it an inter-dimensional being (or beings) that have become attracted by the violent atmosphere pervading Chicago? Do they thrive on this? Is it a sort of omen of an upcoming catastrophe like in Point Pleasant? We can only pray that it is not."

Albert S. Rosales is a friend and colleague. He was born in Cuba, migrating to the US in 1966. Albert became interested in unusual phenomena and UFOs at an early age, but he eventually directed his focus on humanoids, extraterrestrials and other unexplained beings. He began collecting data on such encounters from worldwide sources, beginning in the late 1980s. Albert's well-known humanoid database is continually updated and has resulted in the publication of numerous books.

ROSEMARY ELLEN GUILEY:

Probing the Mystery: A Personal Perspective.

"After all the evidence has been examined and the eyewitnesses interviewed, three big questions remain; how did this happen; why did this happen in the Chicago area; and perhaps most important of all, why did this happen in the first place? It is hard to think that waves of

unexplained phenomena strike for no reason whatsoever; although, when we consider the characteristics of the Trickster, no apparent or logical reason may be the biggest reason of all.

As of this writing, the Chicago wave is still unfolding, and so more information may come to light. Enough events have been documented for a preliminary analysis, and for comparison to the only other similar wave, the Mothman sightings of 1966-67.

To the casual observer, waves of unusual activity, such as cryptid sightings or UFO sightings, seem to erupt suddenly and without apparent cause. They dwindle off or end without apparent cause as well. They remain largely confined to a specific geographic area, though there may be related or spill-over activity in more distant locations.

Researchers who start documenting the events often feel like a door opened to another realm, and "things" started pouring through. It's an explanation that I have long favored myself. John A. Keel, who documented the Mothman sightings, referred to these openings as "windows."

The doorways/portals/windows concept finds support in quantum physics. For example, string theory allows for a multiverse of parallel universes next to or stacked atop one another. Some of them might nearly duplicate the one we exist in, while others might be radically different.

Thus, we can speculate that some of these parallel realities are home to beings, entities, spirits and phenomena that occasionally migrate into our backyard. They don't come from other planets; they are sharing the Earth with us, but in different vibrational spaces.

Earth brims with paranormal and unexplained activity, and always has, according to our oldest records. Most of the time we are not aware of the phenomena, though it goes on around us constantly. When we are in the right place in the right state of mind, we may have an experience.

The Earth also is full of natural "portals," places on the planet where the perceived boundaries between our reality and the "reality of the gods," so to speak, are thin or open. In these places, we have built our sacred shrines and temples. Certain other places with thin boundaries, where the energy is negative and even detrimental to people, are avoided and even called "cursed."

Most of these sensitive areas, or hotspots, fall in the middle, and are host to a wide range of ongoing activity that includes hauntings, poltergeist disturbances, spirit manifestations, strange beings and creatures, mystery lights on the ground and in the sky, aerial activity, and visitations from alien beings.

The dimensional energy of a portal is affected by other factors. One is land energy. There are certain geophysical traits to hotpots. The traits themselves do not guarantee or define a hotspot, yet researchers find many of them in hotspots. Examples are unusual magnetic anomalies that are either positive or negative; soil with a high content of water (such as clay-based), or quartz, iron and magnetite; the presence of strong running underground streams; and the proximity of large rivers and lakes. In folklore, the confluence of rivers is held to make a place especially active, providing a more permeable doorway for the spirit world.

Another factor is the history of events, especially if battles, wars, and disasters have taken place at a location. Such events literally sink their energetic residues into the soil.

And finally, we have human consciousness, which is a wild card. People cart around with them considerable energetic baggage. Some of it is personal, the product of upbringing and life events, and some of it comes from the collective of all human experience; what Carl G. Jung called the collective unconscious. Some of us are natural antennae to the unseen realms, and even trigger phenomena wherever we go; whatever is there, we will stir it up.

We project all of this energy into the environment, and it intermingles with the energy of the unseen realms. We are never discrete observers to anything, natural or paranormal – we are co-creators of, and participants in, all that, "reality" dishes out to us.

When a wave erupts, researchers usually find that the ground zero and environs have a long history of unexplained and paranormal phenomena, or has been home to previous waves, even if they feature different phenomena then the current wave.

The Mothman wave was centered around Point Pleasant, West Virginia in the mid-Ohio River Valley, an area with a considerable haunted history. A lifelong resident I once stayed with for several days said there was not a family in town that didn't have a ghost story or two, or a story about some other kind of weirdness. I have done a great deal of paranormal research in West Virginia over the years, and for a small state, it has an amazing amount of activity, on land and in the skies. The state is full of mountainous contours, mining and abandoned mining sites, and remote areas.

The little town of Point Pleasant sits at the confluence of the Ohio and Kanawa Rivers, marking it, from a folklore perspective, as a highly charged area for the paranormal. A significant battle was fought there in Revolutionary War times. An abandoned TNT plant outside of town contaminated the soil.

Individuals with developed psychic and mediumistic abilities find the energy around Pt. Pleasant to be intense. Perhaps it had the right mix of conditions to become a portal that exploded open for 13 months. But what was the trigger?

In the 1960s, there was a great deal of collective attention focused on outer space. The United States and the Soviet Union were engaged in a space race. We hadn't yet made it to the moon, but the plans were in place. In September 1966, astronaut Gordon Cooper did a spacewalk outside the Gemini XI craft as it orbited the Earth.

UFO reports were popping along, having literally taken off after World War II, and especially the 1947 sighting of flying disc by pilot Kenneth Arnold in Washington State. People around the planet were seeing mystery lights and craft and having bizarre contact experiences. All this collected human energy and focus was bound to have an effect on phenomena, mightily stirring the paranormal pot of simmering ingredients, ready to form. But still; why a backwater place like Pt. Pleasant?

We might consider here the illogical methods of Trickster. Trickster is an archetypal figure in worldwide mythologies through the ages. Trickster is crafty, cunning, deceitful, extremely intelligent, a shapeshifter – and does not play by any rules. Trickster sews mischief and upset.

There is a heavy Trickster undertow to everything paranormal, UFO and cryptid. Whatever powers, the phenomena is intelligent and likes to engage with human consciousness in crazy and even infuriating ways. Things don't make sense. Entities have bizarre appearances and exhibit erratic, bizarre behavior that makes no sense. There are cartoon-like aspects. The phenomena morph and shape shift. Researchers who try to get to the bottom of things wind up, as Keel noted, like dogs chasing their tails. It seems that's the way Trickster likes it.

Perhaps the membrane between realities was extremely thin at Pt. Pleasant in 1966 for unknown reasons, and, like a bubble gum bubble, it popped. Or, it was selected by Trickster.

Inundate a remote area with an onslaught of mind-blowing phenomena that the locals won't know how to handle, and outsiders will dismiss as country bumpkin shenanigans. The stuff is real, but no one anywhere believes it, and for different reasons.

Most of what poured through the Pt. Pleasant portal was UFO related; mystery lights, craft, Men in Black, the "grinning man" Indrid Cold, mysterious messages and predictions, and so on. The winged humanoid given the unfortunate name of Mothman was but one character in a larger cast. Understandably, because of its novelty, Mothman stole the show.

The day the Silver Bridge collapsed in the Ohio River, December 15, 1967, 46 lives were lost, and the portal seemed to collapse as well. Point Pleasant is still an active area, but nowhere near the level of the wave.

Nothing like the Mothman wave has happened anywhere on the planet until 2017, when a flying humanoid wave began in the Chicago area. Fifty years on, how does it compare to Mothman?

We are far more sophisticated, of course, in our technology, and in our approach the topics of alien and extraterrestrial life. We may not know much more about them than we did 50 years ago, but we've improved our research methodologies and open-mindedness. We have armies of knowledgeable lay people eager to examine and investigate.

This time, the activity is in an urban area, raising the potential for more witnesses. The descriptions are not exactly the same as Mothman, but it would be unusual for that to be the case, given the morphing nature of the phenomena, plus the variations in subjective perception on the part of the witnesses. Mothman seemed to be a lone entity, but there may be multiple ones manifesting in Chicago.

The 2017 wave commenced in February with a few reports. Sightings were scattered, but by summertime had picked up in frequency. Chicago has been aided by technology, the internet, and social media, which make information instantly available. The reporting of Mothman activity was heavily reliant upon daily newspapers; information took longer to circulate.

The instant availability of information must certainly be considered as a contributing factor to all aspects of the Chicago wave. The more people who become interested and simply aware, the more people participate in a focus of consciousness which in turn may influence the actual phenomena.

Why is Chicago the ground zero this time? The city certainly has a haunted history behind it, created by its violent, rough and tumble past. It sits on the shore of an immense lake. The presence of water figures heavily in the soil beneath Chicago and the surrounding area: glacial deposits (moraines), a lake plain, outwash plains, valley trains, filled lake basins, river flood plains, and sand dunes. There are enormous quarries in the area, including one of the largest aggregate quarries in the world in Thornton south of Chicago, which produces limestone; another material found in some "portal hotspots."

We need more thorough geological/geophysical research of paranormally active areas to adequately understand the role the Earth itself plays in manifestations.

One significant difference between Mothman and Chicago is the concurrent UFO-related activity. Chicago has not had a comparable upswing in UFOs, ETs, MIBs, and so on; or at least they have not been reported.

Chicago does have one outer space-related factor that may have had a role in the outbreak; a meteor crash into Lake Michigan on February 6, 2017. The fireball was seen in

Illinois and Wisconsin skies. Experts estimate that a 30-pound chunk went into the Lake near Manitowoc, Wisconsin, about one hundred and seventy miles to the north.

I am not suggesting that 'something' piggybacked onto the meteor. The crash of a meteor is an intrusion of material from outer space onto the planet. The crash itself, whether on land or into water, sends shock waves into the environment. Even though this crash was some distance from Chicago, might such shock wave have traveled through the water and had an impact on a portal that was about to open?

Certainly, we also cannot ignore the effects of collective consciousness in either Mothman or Chicago. In the 1960s, we were on edge. We were in a space race, as I mentioned earlier, but we were also on a war tension with the Soviet Union. In 1966, only five years had elapsed since the Bay of Pigs fiasco, a failed US military invasion of Cuba that took us to the brink of nuclear war with the Soviets. That tension was still in the backdrop of world affairs.

In 2017, we found ourselves in similar tension. The presidential election of 2016 had deeply divided the country and shocked the world. We now had a president that many felt might be trigger happy with the nuclear button. The average American was still facing the effects of economic downturn and rising aggression in all areas of life. We were, and still are, fearful.

The manifestations of flying humanoids are frightening to most people. Big, dark and supernatural; many persons interpret them as demonic and evil. Such was the interpretation in some Chicago sightings, especially in the Tinley Park area, where Hispanic witnesses associated the creature with "La Lechuza," a type of demon in Mexican folklore.

"Evil" and "demonic" are not the right terms to apply. The

flying humanoids, including Mothman, have not exhibited a campaign to physically damage, destroy or even possess anyone. Witnesses have certainly feared attack, which is a natural reaction when confronted with a large and terrifying creature.

Rather than assuming that these creatures emanate from some dark hell, where a Lord of Darkness machinates against the souls of human beings, we should look at our own selves in the mirror. The Phenomena – with a capital P – are reflecting back to us what we are projecting outward.

I do not think that these creatures are entirely thought-forms, though thought-form is in the mix. I think they are real entities that exist in alternate realities, the mechanics of which we do not understand, and they interact with the mechanics of this reality, the nature of which is determined and powered by human perception.

These factors make flying humanoids; or any mysterious creature or being, for that matter – a very complicated picture. We want the picture to be simple. They are demons from hell. They are extraterrestrials. They all have a single agenda, and nd so on. Nothing is black and white or sharply defined in the paranormal, however, no matter how hard we try to hammer square pegs into round holes.

Back in the early 1950s, Carl G. Jung addressed this angle in his work, 'Flying Saucers: A Modern Myth Seen in the Skies.' He stated: "In the threatening situation of the world today, when people

are beginning to see that everything is at stake, the projection creating fantasy soars beyond the realm of earthly organizations and powers into the heavens, into interstellar space, where the rulers of human fate, the gods, once had their abode in the planets. (...) Even people who would never have thought that a religious problem could be a serious matter that concerned them personally are beginning to ask themselves fundamental questions. Under these circumstances it would not be at all surprising if those sections of the community who ask themselves nothing were visited by "visions," by a widespread myth seriously believed in by some and rejected as absurd by others." Written more than 60 years ago, it still applies today.

The projection of mass human consciousness does not mean that paranormal phenomena are "all in your head." That, too, is an over simplistic dismissal of the skeptics. Science is still struggling to address the nature of consciousness; what it is, where it "goes," and what it is capable of expressing and creating. The answers can be found in mystical and esoteric traditions and literature. Those concepts, unfortunately, have yet to be anchored into mass consciousness.

As for the paranormal field, including ufology and mysterious creatures; until researchers start factoring in human consciousness, we will make little headway in understanding the phenomena.

We share the planet with other beings and entities, and our "rules of engagement" with them do not fit the logic of this physical reality. Every encounter, every wave, has its unique characteristics, yet fits into broader patterns.

There is one other aspect of flying humanoids that I would like to address; the belief by many that they are "harbingers of doom." This belief especially took hold in mass consciousness after the Mothman wave. There had been predictions of a disaster, and the creature was seen in the vicinity of the Silver Bridge before it collapsed. Since then, there have been sprinklings of flying humanoids seen where other disasters have taken place. Some of them are tenuous.

There are people in the Chicago area now tensed and

waiting for the other shoe to drop. What big disaster is going to befall the Windy City? I do not think that mysterious beings come winging through inter-dimensional portals to usher in disasters. If they are indeed harbingers of doom, they are reflections of our own collective unhappy emotions, fears and anxieties. This is especially the case with flying humanoids. Unlike animal mystery beings and many aliens, they are humanoid, and so are like us, but in an alien and distorted way.

Shadow People – also humanoid in form – often manifest to people whose lives are in turmoil from financial issues, addictions, relationship crises, and major illness. In some cases, witnesses say they show up prior to the onset of a serious problem. Are they warnings – or are they showing up in anticipation of a negative energy feast? I have come to the conclusion that Shadow People are a form taken by Djinn, and they vampirize us of our life force. When people are in states of unhappiness and fear, they make easier targets.

Such may be the case as well with significant manifestations of flying humanoids. We are a fertile feeding ground of dark emotions and fear-generated adrenalin. We have co-created the phenomenon. Perhaps this current wave is yet another lesson in the power of thought, and especially united thought; all discussed in the most ancient of mystical writings, yet something the average person today fails to grasp. Thought creates reality. Thought manifests. Focus on disaster, expect disaster; get disaster.

Rather than cowering beneath the covers waiting for something bad to strike, we should be asking ourselves how to turn things around with our own innate powers of consciousness. We have world prayer days, world meditation days and world healing days, in which people around the planet unite in mass consciousness for a beneficial intention.

Fear unites us, too, and the media artfully fuels those flames daily. Instead of fearing flying humanoids, perhaps we should turn the tables. What would happen if we focused mass positive energy on the phenomena?

We have never tried it. Chicago might be the perfect alchemical alembic for it. Perhaps that is the real purpose behind this latest manifestation of flying humanoids."

EPILOGUE

AT THE TIME this book was published, the sightings of the wing humanoids in Chicago had begun to dramatically wane. The cold weather is steadily approaching, which results in a fewer number of people conducting activities outside. But it has become obvious that the winged humanoids have not presented themselves as earlier reported. It will be interesting to see if a new wave of sightings commences in the upcoming year.

As you have read, there are a number of theories as to the identification of the Chicago Phantom. My personal belief is that there were at least 3 winged beings flying in and around the Chicago metro area and that these sightings will likely continue into the near and distant future. This phenomenon is now a part of the supernatural culture of the great city of Chicago.

I also believe that these flesh and blood winged humanoids were summoned from an alternate reality, and made their way into our world by means of an opened portal. I don't sense that these are evil entities, but they do possess abilities that are difficult for us to comprehend. I haven't perceived a specific connection between the witnesses and their sightings, other than they were given a unique opportunity to observe an otherworldly anomaly.

This historical group of sightings in the Chicago area will be examined by enthusiasts in the future. I have every intention of seeking more evidence related to this phenomenon, and hopefully find answers.

The research and investigation of cryptids is a devotion that many of us enjoy. We live in an uncommon and decisive era for the exploration of the unexplained. It will require a willingness to be steadfast and open-minded, because the presence of the Mothman dynasty is destined to continue.

ABOUT THE AUTHOR

Lon Strickler is a Fortean researcher, author, and publisher of the syndicated 'Phantoms and Monsters' blog. He began the blog in 2005, which has steadily grown in popularity and is read daily by tens of thousands of paranormal enthusiasts, investigators and those seeking the truth. His research and reports have been featured on hundreds of online media sources. Several of these published reports have been presented on various television segments, including The History Channel's 'Ancient Aliens,' Syfy's 'Paranormal Witness', 'Fact or Faked: Paranormal Files,' and Destination America's 'Monsters and Mysteries in America.'

He has been interviewed on hundreds of radio & online broadcasts, including multiple guest appearances on 'Coast to Coast AM.' He was also featured on Destination America's 'Monsters and Mysteries in America' television show for 'The

Sykesville Monster' episode. Lon has written eight books and is currently the host of Arcane Radio on Beyond Explanation YouTube channel.

Lon was born and raised in south central Pennsylvania, near the Gettysburg National Military Park and Battlefield. After living in the Baltimore, MD metro area for forty years, he eventually moved back to his hometown in 2016.

Alien Disclosure: Experiencers Expose Reality

Printed in Great Britain
by Amazon